The First Book of

Personal Computing

R E L A T E D   T I T L E S

*For the retailer nearest you, or to order directly from the publisher, call
800-257-5755. International orders telephone 609-461-6500.*

The First Book of

Personal Computing

W.E. Wang and Joe Kraynak

HOWARD W. SAMS & COMPANY

A Division of Macmillan, Inc.

FIRST EDITION

THIRD PRINTING — 1991

International Standard Book Number: 0-672-27313-6
Library of Congress Catalog Card Number: 90-60957

Acquisitions Editor: *Richard K. Swadley*
Development Editors: *Wendy Ford and Marjorie Hopper*
Manuscript Editor: *Albright Communications, Incorporated*
Illustrator: *Tami Hughes*
Cover Artist: *Held & Diedrich Design*
Indexer: *Hilary Adams*
Production: *Sally Copenhaver, Denny Hager, Jodi Jensen, Lori Lyons, Dennis Sheehan, Bruce D. Steed, Mary Beth Wakefield*

Printed in the United States of America

Contents

vi

vii

ix

Introduction

Learning to use a computer is not difficult. Don't listen to people who say otherwise. They'll tell you all about languages and commands, and ask you about your chips and bits and bytes in an attempt to appear superior. Don't fall for it; all that information is good to know, but you don't need to learn everything at once. Learn a small block of information, then start building.

This book helps you build your house of knowledge. It presents basic chunks of information in each chapter, introducing a specific topic about computers. Each chapter shows you how the computer can make your life easier and gives you a basic understanding of computer operations. You learn the terminology in an understandable context.

We take you on a tour of the computer world, showing you all its magnificent splendor, pointing out the programs and features that help you perform your work, revealing what's available in the market and how to make the most of it. We show you the basic steps required to run a computer and the various ways to perform those steps.

On the way, we also point out some of the limitations of computers and programs, some of the pitfalls you may encounter, and what to watch out for when you're shopping for computer equipment. You learn how to prevent some of the common problems that beginners face when they first start working with computers and where to go for help. We even throw in a few secrets along the way.

When you first start using a computer, remember to dive in slowly. You've already taken the right first step by buying this First Book. The second step is to approach the computer in a relaxed atmosphere and practice.

One more thing—have fun! Too many people limit their learning by being afraid to play on the computer. Play, experiment, test the limits, and you will soon find yourself flying through your daily tasks.

Acknowledgments

Although all books are team projects, this book required a special team —one consisting of both novices and experts. The novices offered their insights into what beginners need to know, the experts supplied the necessary information.

Special thanks to Wendy Ford for getting us all together for this project. Her encouragement and wisdom kept the book moving over some pretty rough terrain.

Thanks to Marj Hopper for coordinating the project. Without Marj, this book would still be a heap of paper spread across several desks...in a couple of states.

Thanks to Nancy Albright, our manuscript editor, who not only tightened up the text and fixed our language errors, but who also asked important questions that cleared up some of the more technical passages.

Finally, thanks to all the people who gave us the time to write. First, thanks to Bill Gladstone, Wonder Book Agent, who knows more people in the computer industry than most people know in the rest of the world. Another bow of thanks goes to Herbert and Ruth Wang, whose bewilderment over personal computers helped shape the focus of this book. And Cecie Kraynak, Joe's spouse, who cleaned, cooked, and amused the kids for six weeks straight, while Joe wrote.

Trademarks

All terms mentioned in this book that are known to be trademarks or service marks are listed below. In addition, terms suspected of being trademarks or service marks have been appropriately capitalized. Howard W. Sams & Company cannot attest to the accuracy of this information. Use of a term in this book should not be regarded as affecting the validity of any trademark or service mark.

1-2-3 and Freelance Plus are registered trademarks of Lotus Development.

4th Dimension is a registered trademark of Acius Corporation.

Consulair Development System is a registered trademark of Consulair Development.

CorelDraw is a registered trademark of Corel Systems Corporation.

DesignStudio and Ready,Set,Go! are registered trademarks of Letraset.

FileMaker Pro, MacDraw, and MacPaint are registered trademarks of Claris Corporation.

FoxPro and FoxBase+/Mac are registered trademarks of Fox Software.

Framework III, Full Impact, dBASE, dBASE II, dBASE III, dBASE III Plus, and dBASE IV are registered trademarks of Ashton-Tate.

IBM and PC DOS are registered trademarks of International Business Machines Corporation.

MemoryMate is a registered trademark of Broderbund Software.

PageMaker is a registered trademark of Aldus Corporation.

Paradox, Turbo Pascal, Turbo C, Turbo Assembler, Quattro Pro, and Reflex are registered trademarks of Borland International.

PC Tools Deluxe and MacTools Deluxe are registered trademarks of Central Point Software.

PC-File is a registered trademark of ButtonWare.

PFS: First Publisher, PFS: First Choice, and Harvard Graphics are registered trademarks of Software Publishing Corporation.

Q&A, THINK C, and THINK Pascal are registered trademarks of Symantec Corporation.

Quark XPress is a registered trademark of Quark, Inc.

xiii

Chapter 1

Making a Personal Computer Work for You

In This Chapter

▶ *How a computer works for you*

▶ *Using the computer to cut down on the time you spend reworking*

▶ *Why a computer performs some tasks faster and more efficiently than you can*

▶ *The five basic functions of any computer program*

A computer is a tool. It doesn't think up ideas for advertising campaigns or deduce scientific theories. It simply performs three very basic tasks. First, it records and stores your work so you don't have to re-create the entire piece to incorporate a single change. Second, it performs repetitive tasks tirelessly and with great precision. Third, it follows your commands, allowing you to customize and design your work so it meets your exact needs.

These three features make personal computers useful tools for writing letters and memos, balancing checkbooks and budgets, keeping track of accounts receivables and mailing lists, and plotting stock market information or other trends. If you can perform a task using a pencil, some paper, and a calculator, chances are that you can perform the same task more efficiently and accurately using a computer.

Think of the computer in terms of the rework it saves you. In the past, if you found a typo in a letter, a chart, or a report you just wrote, you had three choices: erase it, paint it with white-out—if appearance didn't count—or retype the entire document. With a computer, however, you don't have to retype the entire page; you correct only the typo, fix only what's broken. You print the final version only after you approve of its final form.

Many computer programs offer standard features that perform the more common repetitive tasks, such as searching for a word or record, replacing a term throughout a document, sorting records into groups, and organizing and updating lists.

Finally, a computer also saves you design and printing costs. In the past, if you wanted to put together an attractive brochure or publish a report, you had to enlist the aid of a graphics artist and a typesetter. If you were determined to do it yourself, you had to do some pretty fancy work with rub-off type or stencils. Now, with a graphics program and a good dot matrix printer, you can create a wide variety of high-quality publications without leaving your desk and without paying someone else to do it.

Table 1-1 lists a few of the tasks you may now be performing manually and the computer alternatives.

Table 1-1. The Computer Alternatives

Task	Manual Method	Computer Alternative
Writing letters	Typewriter	Word processor
Balancing a budget	Calculator	Spreadsheet
Storing names and addresses	Rolodex	Database
Generating purchase orders	Calculator, typewriter	Accounting program

The Five Basic Functions

As you can see, the computer can perform a wide variety of tasks, depending on your requirements and on the programs you have access to.

Despite this variation, all programs perform the following five basic functions:

▶ Storing data

▶ Retrieving data

▶ Editing data

▶ Displaying data

▶ Printing data

Storing Data

A computer can store a lot of data in very little space by storing it on *magnetic disks* rather than on paper. These disks are similar to cassette tapes. A single disk can hold several chapters of a book. A small box of disks can hold an entire filing cabinet of work.

As shown in Figure 1-1, the disk storage system is structured very much like a filing cabinet. Each document you create is stored in a *file*, and several files are stored in a *directory*. You'll learn more about this in Chapter 3.

3

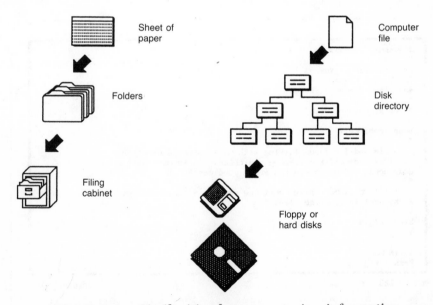

Sheet of paper

Folders

Filing cabinet

Computer file

Disk directory

Floppy or hard disks

Figure 1-1. Similarities between storing information manually and with a computer.

Retrieving Data

Once you've stored information in your system, you can use the computer to find it quickly. Instead of flipping through a stack of folders to find a file, tell the computer what to look for, and it does the rest, searching for information that matches your instructions. Finding information is so easy, you won't hesitate to look for it. This reduces both the time wasted searching through files *and* the alternatives: relying on memory or stab-in-the-dark guesswork. More precise data retrieval plus more efficient time management minus reduced human error equals improved productivity.

Editing Data

4

When you retrieve data, the computer displays an electronic version of it, as shown in Figure 1-2. You can then modify this data by adding, deleting, or rearranging information on the screen. Some programs even let you move an entire section of a document from one place to another. When the data is exactly as you want it, you can save the revised version to disk and retrieve it for the next editing session.

```
January·31,··1990¶
¶
Ms.··Jennifer·G.··Young↓
The·Weldon·Company↓
430·Black·Canyon·Highway↓
Mail·Stop·33↓
Phoenix,·Arizona·85082¶
¶
Dear·Jennifer:¶
¶
→    Jim·and·I·enjoyed·talking·with·you·yesterday·about·the·
services·Oberfeld·and·Company·can·offer.··It·appears·that·
your·needs·and·our·strengths·are·a·good·match.··¶
¶
→    I'll·call·you·in·the·next·few·days·to·discuss·when·we·
might·meet·to·finalize·plans.¶
¶
Sincerely,¶
¶
¶
Katie·Magill↓
President↓

                                                         ┌CH5.DOC┐
P62 D3 L23 C10    {¶}              ?              Microsoft Word
```

Figure 1-2.   An electronic version of a letter displayed on screen. (Reprinted, by permission, from Kate Barnes, The Best Book of Microsoft Word 5.)

Displaying Data

The computer can display the same information in different ways to help you analyze it. If you're a teacher, for example, you can chart your students' grades on a spreadsheet to help you determine averages at report-card time. If you want to see more clearly how your students are progressing, use the computer to graph the same information.

Printing Data

Your printer is much more versatile than even the fanciest typewriter, because it takes its direction from the computer. . . and the computer can provide a wide variety of instructions. For example, if you need to print several copies of a memo, simply tell your computer which memo you want to print and how many copies you need, and the computer sends the information on to the printer.

Some programs even offer a *merge* feature that lets you insert information from one source into a form letter from another source and print out the result.

Clearing the First Hurdle

Learning to use a computer takes patience. The trick is to approach the computer in a relaxed atmosphere. When you sit down at your computer for the first time, have a brief task that you commonly perform manually. Then, read, play, experiment, and read some more. You'll learn the material without even trying, performing tasks faster every day.

5

What You've Learned

In this chapter, you learned that the computer can help you perform everyday tasks faster and easier. In the next chapter, you see what it is about the inner workings of the computer that makes it so useful. But before you do that, review some of what we discussed here:

▶ Computers are problem-solving tools.

▶ Computers take some of the drudgery out of your daily routine.

▶ Every computer program performs five basic functions.

▶ Learning to use a computer is easy.

6

Chapter 2

The Equipment You Need

In This Chapter

▶ *The various components that make up a computer system*

▶ *The function of each component and how all the components work together to perform real tasks*

▶ *Computer terminology that helps you understand and talk with computer salespeople and service technicians*

▶ *Basic concepts that give you a clear understanding of how the computer operates*

If you had to assemble your own computer from scratch, you'd have a long shopping list. First, you would need the following *hardware*, as shown in Figure 2-1. These are the parts that break when you drop them:

Input Device. A *keyboard* or *mouse* enables you to enter information into the computer and commands to tell the computer what to do.

Central Processing Unit (CPU). This device processes the information you enter, so that the other parts of the computer system can understand the information.

Disk Drive. This device reads information from disks (so you can run programs), stores the information you enter onto a disk, and retrieves information when you want to work on it.

Output Device. This device translates the information into a usable form (a video monitor, a printer, or a modem).

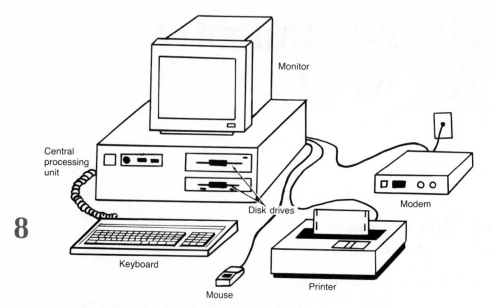

8

Figure 2-1.   The hardware required for you to operate.

You also need *software*, the instructions that tell your computer what to do. You need two types of software—*operating system software* and an *application program*.

The operating system software is a go-between program; it lets the various pieces of hardware talk to each other and lets your computer use an application program. The application program is the software that helps you do your job, such as word processing or balancing your books. This is the software that gets all the glory.

Both types of software come on disks. You usually use the system software to start up your computer at the beginning of a day or work session. Then when you want to perform a particular task, run the application program that you bought for it. You learn more about this software in Chapter 4.

The last items on your shopping list are blank disks, several of them, to store your precious creations.

How the Components Work Together

A computer operates very much like a cassette recorder. With the latter, you enter information by speaking into a microphone (the input device). The cassette recorder (central processing unit) translates these sound waves into electrical impulses that are recorded (stored) on a magnetic cassette tape. When you want to hear what you recorded, you can use the cassette recorder to translate the magnetic impulses from the tape back into electrical impulses. These impulses are then amplified and sent to a speaker (the output device) that makes the sounds audible.

With a computer, the keyboard lets you enter electrical impulses, which the central processing unit translates and stores temporarily in its electronic memory, as shown in Figure 2-2. This information is sent to your monitor so you can see what you're doing. In other words, if you're creating a document, it actually consists of electrical impulses. When you edit the document, you're essentially changing an electronic draft.

9

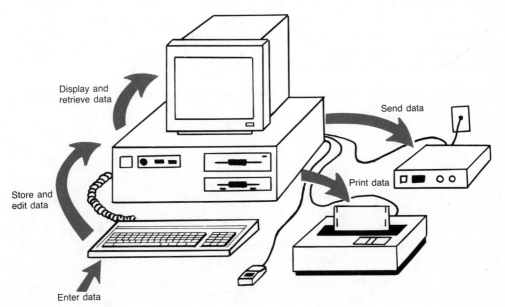

Figure 2-2. How the computer system works.

When you've finished revising and rearranging this electronic version, store it on a magnetic disk. Whenever you want to work on the document, insert the magnetic disk and play back the document on screen.

If you want to print the document, play it back to your printer, where the electrical impulses are translated into characters and symbols. You can even use an output device called a *modem* to send the document through the telephone lines to a colleague in another state or country.

Disk Drives

10

Before your computer can do anything, it needs a set of instructions to orient it and tell it what to do. These instructions are stored magnetically on a disk and are referred to as *programs*. To read the information off the disks, the computer uses a disk drive that converts the magnetic signals from the disk into electronic signals that the computer can understand.

In addition to reading information from disks, the disk drive is responsible for writing information onto disks. For example, if you type a letter and want to save it for later, tell the disk drive to write the letter to the disk. (More about this later.)

There are two types of disk drives: the *floppy disk* drive and the *hard disk* drive.

Floppy Disks

Floppy disks are the disks you insert into your computer's disk drive, and owe their name to their early form. They *were* floppy—you could bend them. Now, there are two kinds of floppy disks. The early version (the 5 1/4-inch disk) is still floppy, but the newer (3 1/2-inch disk) is a stiff plastic card, as shown in Figure 2-3.

Two characteristics describe floppy disks: *size* and *capacity*. The size of a disk refers to its physical measurements (its dimensions) and dictates what kind of disk drive it fits into. The capacity of a disk refers to the maximum amount of information the disk can hold. This capacity is measured in *kilobytes (K)* and *megabytes (M)*. Each *byte* consists of 8 *bits* and is used to store a single character. A kilobyte is

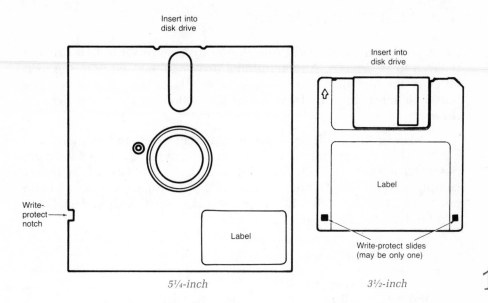

Figure 2-3.   The two types of floppy disks.

1,024 bytes—1,024 characters. Maximum is important here. For your disk to work properly, you should use only up to 90% of a disk's capacity.

A disk's capacity depends on whether it stores information on one side (single-sided) or both sides (double-sided) and how much information it lets you cram in a given amount of space (the disk's density). Table 2-1 shows the types of floppy disks that are available and how much information they hold.

Table 2-1. Floppy Disks

Size	Type	Storage Capacity
5 ¼"	Double-sided/double-density (DS/DD)	360K
5 ¼"	High-density or quad-density (HD or QD)	1.2M
3 ½"	Single-sided/double-density (SS/DD)	400K
3 ½"	Double-sided/double-density (DS/DD)	800K
3 ½"	High-density or quad-density (HD or QD)	1.44M

The Floppy Disk Drive

Every computer has at least one floppy disk drive. This first drive is referred to as *drive A*. Any additional drives are labeled with the next letter in the alphabet. For example, if you have two disk drives, the top or leftmost drive is drive A and the bottom or rightmost drive is *drive B*.

Because floppy disks come in different sizes and capacities, a given disk drive can handle only a particular type of disk. Older computers have one or two 5 ¼-inch floppy disk drives. Many of the newer computers have two disk drives: one for 5 ¼-inch floppy disks and one for 3 ½-inch disks. Table 2-2 shows the various disk drives available and the types of disks each can handle.

Table 2-2. Floppy Disk Drives

Disk Size	Floppy Disk Drive	Disk Capacities
5 ¼"	Double-density	360K
5 ¼"	High-density	1.2M, 360K
3 ½"	Double-density	800K, 400K
3 ½"	High-density	1.44M, 800K, 400K

In general, a disk drive can read disks that are equal to or less than its own capacity. A high-capacity disk drive can read low-capacity disks, but the reverse will not work—a low-capacity disk drive cannot read high-capacity disks.

> ▶ **Note:** Although a high-capacity disk drive can write information on a low-capacity disk, a low-capacity disk drive may not be able to read the disk.

The Convenience of a Hard Disk

The hard disk acts like a giant floppy disk that's permanently installed in the computer. Although the hard disk is not an essential component, it does make life a lot easier.

Even the smallest hard disk can store large amounts of data. For example, a 20M hard disk (the smallest) can store the same amount of data as sixty 5 ¼-inch, double-density floppy disks or twenty-five 3 ½-inch, double-density disks.

Each hard disk may be divided into several "disk drives" to make it more manageable. For example, you may have two floppy disk drives, A and B, and three hard disk drives—C, D, and E. Don't be fooled; the three hard disk drives apply to the same disk. Whenever you tell your computer to read data that's stored on a disk, you need to enter one of these letters to tell the computer which disk drive the disk is in.

If you don't have a hard disk, you have to *swap* disks—eject one floppy disk from the disk drive and insert another. Every time your computer needs information that's not on a disk in one of your disk drives, it displays a message like "Please insert system disk into drive A" or "Please insert program disk into drive B."

13

The Monitor

When you're using a computer, you need to see what you're doing. That's where the *monitor* comes in. The monitor is a lot like a TV screen; it displays electronic signals in a recognizable form, in this case as characters, numbers, or even graphics symbols. The monitor goes by many names; you'll also hear it referred to as a *screen* and a *CRT (Cathode Ray Tube)*.

The little blinking dot or line on the monitor, is called the *cursor*. With it you move around the screen, enter and delete information, and choose items displayed on your screen. If you're typing a line of text, for example, the cursor moves from left to right across your screen. Each time you type a letter or number, the letter or number seems to pop up out of the cursor, and the cursor moves to the next space.

If you do a lot of work with a pencil and paper, it'll take some getting used to working on a computer and seeing your creation on screen. But with some practice, you'll be moving the cursor around about as quickly and easily as you can move the tip of your pencil.

Two devices let you move the cursor and manipulate the information on your monitor: the keyboard and the mouse. The keyboard is the more essential of the two. The mouse is an optional device that lets you move the cursor around the screen a little more easily.

Using a Keyboard

A computer keyboard has many more keys than a typewriter keyboard (see Figure 2-4). Typewriters have keys for typing characters, numbers, and symbols, and a few keys, such as the Tab key and the Backspace key, for moving to where you want to type.

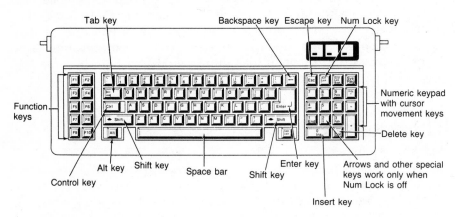

Figure 2-4.   An example of a computer keyboard.

The computer keyboard has all of those keys plus many special ones.

Cursor Movement Keys

Cursor movement keys do just that; they move the cursor around the screen and let you enter information and commands. These keys appear as arrows on your keyboard and include the up/down and left/right arrow keys, the Page Up and Page Down keys, and the Home and End keys. The Home and End keys move the cursor quickly, to the beginning and end, respectively, of either a screen or a document.

The cursor movement keys are located on a separate keypad. Some keyboards have a special keypad exclusively for the arrow keys.

On other keyboards, the cursor movement keys are located on the numeric keypad.

Editing Keys

The editing keys, *Ins* and *Del* (Insert and Delete) let you insert and delete information. The Del key gobbles up characters, one by one. To delete a character, move the cursor to the space before or after the character (depending on the program) and press the Del (Delete) key.

The Ins key is a *toggle* that switches the cursor from Insert to Overstrike mode and vice versa. Normally, if you move the cursor to a place in your document and start typing, you insert information without deleting existing characters. If you press Ins, you switch to Overstrike mode; anything you type now, types *over* any existing text. Usually, the program you're using displays the mode you're using on screen.

15

The Numeric Keypad

The *numeric keypad* contains ten number keys and four keys for entering math symbols. These keys also act as cursor movement keys when the Num Lock key is not activated.

> ▶ **Tip:** If you plan on entering a lot of numbers, consider getting a keyboard that has a separate set of cursor movement keys. Otherwise, you need to press Num Lock every time you want to type a number.

Function Keys

Function keys, commonly referred to as F keys (F1, F2, F3, etc.), are the ten keys on the left side of your keyboard or the 12 keys at the top, depending on your keyboard's configuration. Use these keys to enter commands quickly. For example, a program might use the F5 key to delete a line of text or the F4 key to type a word in boldface. The way the function keys are used depends on the application software you are running.

Other Special Keys

In addition to the groups of special keys mentioned above are several individual keys—*Esc*, *Alt*, and *Ctrl*:

The Esc key is usually used to return to the previous screen—that is, it lets you *escape* from the present screen.

Alt (alternative) gives you an alternate keyboard. For example, if you hold down the Alt key and type **139** on the numeric keyboard, you get this: ï.

Just as you can use the Alt key to make your character keys type different characters, you can use the Ctrl (Control) key to make your command keys enter different commands.

16

Combination Keys

In addition to all these keys, you can press a combination of keys to get even more out of your keystrokes. For example, you might press the F4 key as mentioned above to type a word in bold, but if you hold down the Ctrl (Control) key and press F4, your program may check the spelling in a document!

It takes a while to learn the combinations, but with a little practice, you'll be using these combination keys as naturally as you press the Shift key to type a capital letter.

Using a Mouse

The mouse owes its name to its physical appearance; it looks like a little creature with a tail (the cable that connects it to your central processing unit). The mouse is designed to make moving the cursor more natural—a little more like using a pencil. Instead of pressing keys to move around the screen, you slide the mouse on a flat surface in the direction you want the cursor to move.

When you use the mouse, the screen may display both a cursor and a mouse pointer. Most programs include *menus*, which are lists of options you can choose from to enter commands. If your system is set up for a mouse, you can use the mouse to point to items on the menu. To select an item, press a button on the mouse; this is called *clicking* on an item. You can also *double-click* on an item (press the mouse button twice in quick succession) to enter a different command. One of the most helpful features of the mouse is that you can use it to *drag* items displayed on your screen across the screen. To drag, hold down the mouse button while you slide the mouse. When the item is positioned where you want it, release the button, and you're done. Artists find this feature most useful, because it lets them use the mouse to draw sketches.

The Central Processing Unit (CPU)   17

The central processing unit controls the operation of the computer by

- ▶ Running the programs that are stored on disk
- ▶ Processing the information you enter
- ▶ Controlling the output of information to your monitor, printer, and modem (if you're using one)

The CPU performs these tasks by using two types of memory: *RAM (Random Access Memory)* and *ROM (Read Only Memory)*.

RAM (Random Access Memory)

Whenever you *load* a program into your computer or play back one of your creations, the computer reads the information from the disk and copies it into its Random Access Memory. It then uses the information in RAM to interpret and carry out the commands you enter.

RAM is actually made up of several electronic components called *chips* that store information electronically. If you load a document into RAM and then turn off your computer, RAM "forgets" the document. That's why it's so important to store information magnetically on disks.

So why not just use disks? The main reason is speed. If the computer had to play back instructions from your program disk every time you entered a command, it would take forever. RAM makes it a lot easier for your computer to read and carry out instructions.

> ▶ **Tip:** If you're shopping for a computer, you need to know how much RAM a computer has. RAM is measured in kilobytes. Remember, a kilobyte is 1,024 bytes—1,024 characters. You must make sure that the computer has enough RAM to store the program you want to run, plus enough room to hold the electronic document you'll be working on. We look at this more in Chapter 13.

18 *ROM (Read Only Memory)*

Unlike RAM, ROM doesn't forget—it's a more stable memory, so you can't do much with it. ROM's main function is to carry out the central processing unit's management functions. Most of ROM is used by the ROM BIOS (**B**asic **I**nput/**O**utput **S**ystem) that provides the instructions telling the CPU how to communicate with your keyboard, printer, and monitor. The remaining ROM is free space that you can use as you get more advanced—don't worry about it for now.

How Fast Is Fast Enough?

Like people, some computers work faster than others. With some computers, you can enter a command, go get a cup of coffee, drink it, and then come back to watch the computer finish up. Other computers are so fast that they can get you into trouble if you're not careful. They can check the spelling of a 50-page document in less than a minute, but they can erase the same document even faster. That's not to say that speed is bad—the faster, the better. You don't want to have to wait a minute or more for your computer to catch up with you every time you enter a command.

The speed of a computer is measured in *megahertz (MHz)* and is related to the model number of the *microprocessor* you're using. The microprocessor is the brain behind your computer, an integrated circuit that contains an entire CPU on a single chip—we discuss it later. The earliest microprocessor for IBM and compatible computers was the 8088, which ran at 4.77 MHz. More modern microprocessors, such as the 80386 (referred to as the 386), can operate at speeds exceeding 30 MHz, and they're getting faster every day.

To give you some idea of how megahertz translates into seconds, Table 2-3 shows the speed for three common microprocessors.

Table 2-3. Time Needed to Add 10,000 Numbers

Microprocessor	Speed (MHz)	Time Needed
8086	8 MHz	128 seconds
80286	12 MHz	32 seconds
80386	20 MHz	8 seconds

19

Seeing It in Print

When you're done creating and perfecting your work, you will surely want to share it with someone. You can do this in either of two ways: you can print out a *hard copy* of your work, or, if you have a modem, you can send it over the phone lines to someone else who has a computer and a modem.

The most common way to share your work is to print the information stored in your computer, or on a disk, to paper. Depending on your need and budget, you can choose from a variety of printers.

If you're deciding which printer to buy, keep a few things in mind:

Paper Size. Some printers handle the standard 8 1/2-by-11-inch paper very well, but are not suited for wider paper. If you plan to print wide spreadsheets, get a printer that can handle the job.

Automatic Feed. If you need to print several pages continuously, get a printer with automatic feed. These printers have a *tractor feed* that pulls special computer paper through the printer automatically.

Fonts. If you plan on printing newsletters or creating your own greeting cards, make sure the printer supports the fonts and type styles you want to use.

Quality. Several printers can print in two different qualities: *draft quality* and *near-letter quality (NLQ)*. In draft mode, the printer prints a low-quality draft quickly. In NLQ mode, it prints a higher quality copy more slowly.

Dot Matrix Printers

The dot matrix printer is the most common and versatile printer. The characters it prints consist of a series of dots arranged in a pattern. Since these dots can be arranged in any number of patterns, you can use this printer to print graphics images and a variety of type styles.

20   The quality of print you'll get out of a dot matrix printer varies, depending on the printer and how many *dots per inch (dpi)* it prints. (The resolution of dot matrix printers can range from 30 x 60 to 360 x 360 dpi.) The more dpi, the more solid each character will look.

Daisywheel Printers

If all you're ever going to use your printer for is printing out characters and numbers, the daisywheel printer is great. It provides a printout that looks just as though you typed it on a typewriter. The only drawback is that this printer cannot print graphics such as bar charts and pie graphs.

Inkjets and Plotters

For printing graphs, charts, or diagrams, inkjet printers or plotters are excellent. The inkjet printer works by spraying ink onto a page. The plotter functions like a robotic hand that draws on a sheet of paper. While not common for use in the home or for most offices, either of these printers is a welcome addition to drafting or marketing departments, where clean, even lines are a must.

Laser Printers

Laser printers are the king daddies of the printer world. They have the versatility of the dot matrix printer and the quality of the inkjet all rolled into one. Because of this sophistication, they have virtually revolutionized the publishing business—and are the most expensive.

Although the name suggests that laser printers use some exotic laser technology, a laser printer actually works like a photocopy machine.

Computers That Talk Through the Phone Lines

21

Through the use of *modems*, two computers can share information over the phone lines—and the computers don't even have to be compatible! One person in Atlanta can transfer information from an IBM computer to a Macintosh computer in Los Angeles. Because modems work with any computer, many people use modems to work at home and transfer their data to their office computer at the end of the day.

A modem transfers information at a certain speed, measured in *baud* or *bits-per-second (bps)*. The maximum speed is referred to as a modem's *baud rate*, typically 300, 1,200, 2,400, and 9,600. The higher the baud rate, the faster a modem can talk.

> ▶ **Tip:** A modem can transmit data at any of several speeds but can only receive data at its maximum rate. For example, to transfer data between two computers, one with a baud rate of 2,400 and one with a baud rate of 9,600, the maximum speed is 2,400 baud. Since the maximum speed depends on the slowest modem, buy the fastest modem you can afford.

What You've Learned

If you're pretty comfortable with the information in this section, you're in good shape. This chapter contains most of the basics and a lot of the terminology you'll encounter when working with computers. Let's look at some of the more important concepts you learned here:

▶ The computer consists of four basic components: an input device, a processing device, a storage device, and an output device.

▶ The monitor lets you see what you're doing on screen.

▶ The keyboard and mouse let you enter information and commands into your computer.

▶ Random Access Memory (RAM) is a temporary, electronic storage facility for programs and files.

▶ The speed of your computer is measured in megahertz and is related to the model number of your microprocessor.

▶ You must save the information stored in RAM to disk in order to protect your work.

▶ The hard disk gives you more storage room, so you don't have to swap disks.

▶ You can choose from a variety of printers, depending on your needs and your budget.

▶ Computers can transfer data over phone lines through the use of modems.

Interacting with Your Computer

In This Chapter

▶ *Starting up your computer*

▶ *Running the programs that help you do your work*

▶ *Creating files to store your work*

▶ *Organizing the files you create*

▶ *What an operating system is and how you can make it easier to use*

▶ *Using the operating system to perform daily tasks*

▶ *Viewing a list of what's on a disk*

▶ *Insuring your work against damage*

No matter how basic or sophisticated a computer is, it can't do more than warm its chips until it receives a set of instructions to follow. It needs a game plan—the software—to orient it to the tasks it will be performing.

Remember to use your computer to perform a specific task, you need two types of software: operating system software and applications software. The operating system software starts up your computer; it gets all the parts of your computer communicating with one another. You can consider it the main program. Applications software consists of *sub-programs* that work within the operating system. It's these programs that let you create electronic documents and use your computer to perform specific tasks, such as typing a report or balancing your accounts. Figure 3-1 shows how the different software programs work together.

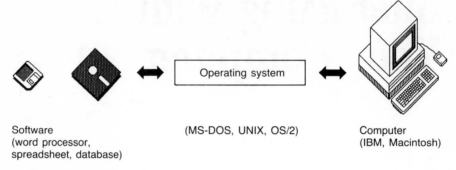

Software
(word processor,
spreadsheet, database)

(MS-DOS, UNIX, OS/2)

Computer
(IBM, Macintosh)

Figure 3-1.   An operating system lets your computer run programs like word processors, spreadsheets, and databases.

24

Starting Up Your Computer

If you turn on your computer without an operating system disk loaded, you are greeted by a blank screen or a screen that tells you to insert the operating system disk into one of the disk drives. The computer simply needs more information. So before flipping on the power switch, be sure that your operating system software is in one of the disk drives.

If you purchase a computer with a hard disk drive, the dealer may already have *installed* (copied) the operating system on the hard disk. When you turn on the power, your computer reads the instructions off the hard disk and displays a screen you can use to start running your applications programs. This startup procedure is referred to as *booting* the system.

If you have a floppy disk drive, you must load the operating system disk into drive A (the top or leftmost drive) before you turn on your computer. The disk drive makes funny noises as it reads the instructions, but after a moment or so, the operating system will be loaded into RAM, and you can remove the disk from the disk drive.

> ▶ **Tip:** You usually need only one operating system for your computer; your choice depends on the computer you have and on the applications programs you want to run. The most popular operating systems for IBM and compatible computers are DOS (**D**isk **O**perating **S**ystem—PC DOS and MS-DOS are two versions), OS/2, and Xenix (the IBM version of UNIX). Macintosh computers use an operating system called System 7.0 or the Macintosh version of UNIX called AU/X. You'll hear these names thrown around a lot, but all you have to do is make sure you have an operating system that works on your computer and can run the applications programs that you want to run. Most of the examples in this chapter focus on DOS, because it's somewhat more difficult, and if you understand a little about DOS, you'll have no trouble understanding other operating systems.

25

Entering Commands with Prompts and Menus

When you start up your computer, the first thing you will see on screen is a menu or a *prompt*, indicating that the computer is now ready to accept a command. With the DOS operating system, the prompt typically consists of a letter followed by a colon (:) and an angle bracket: A:> or C:>. (Sometimes the prompt does not include the colon: C>.)

The letter represents the currently active disk drive. If you type a command, the operating system carries out the command on the disk that's in the active drive. To change the active drive, just type the letter that represents the drive, type a colon, and then press the Enter key. For example, if A:> is displayed on screen and you want to use drive B, type **b:** next to the A:> prompt and press Enter.

After you start up your computer, you need to enter some command to continue. A Macintosh computer prompts you to "Load Your Program Disk" into one of the drives, whereas DOS displays a prompt that asks you to enter a date or that indicates which drive is active.

With a Macintosh computer, the operating system is *menu-driven*, meaning that you enter commands by choosing a command from a menu

[handwritten margin note: How can you change from an A drive to a B without changing disk?]

of available commands. When you start up a Macintosh, the screen displays a menu bar at the top of the screen and at least one picture (*icon*) of a disk, as shown in Figure 3-2. To activate a drive, use the mouse to point at one of the disk icons, and then press the mouse button (click on the icon). Once the disk drive is made active, you can choose commands from the menus to perform a specific task.

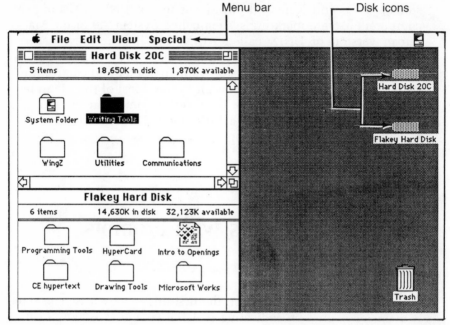

Figure 3-2. A Macintosh screen.

> **Note:** You will see later that there are ways to turn DOS into a menu-driven program, making it work a lot like a Macintosh.

Preparing Blank Disks

One of the most important tasks that your operating system performs is the *formatting* or *initializing* of a disk. This process organizes your disk so that your type of computer can locate and read information from the disk quickly and easily. The initializing process for the Macintosh computers also lets you name the disk so the name appears on screen within the icon.

Before you begin using your computer to create documents or reports, or anything else you might want to keep, make sure that you have a blank, formatted disk available, or you won't be able to save your work. To format a disk using DOS, insert it in the disk drive and type **format a:** following the prompt.

Running Applications Programs

Applications programs translate the power of the operating system into a language that you can understand so you can use your computer to perform real tasks, such as tracking inventory and printing newsletters. We look at what these programs can do in the next few chapters, but for now, let's look at how you run these programs on your computer.

Before you can start using the computer to perform a given task, insert the disk for the applications program into the active drive and enter a command to run the program. For example, if you're using an IBM computer and **A:** is displayed on screen, insert the applications program disk into drive A and then type the command to run the program. For example, type **ws** to run the word processing program WordStar.

27

Understanding Files

Once you run the applications program, you won't see much of your operating system anymore—it fades into the background as the applications program takes over.

When you run most applications programs, the first thing you see is a screen that gives you several options from which to choose. The first option you need to concern yourself with is the option to create a file. When you create a file, you're essentially creating a receptacle for whatever document or project you're about to start.

Creating a file consists of giving the file a unique name that keeps it separate from other files on the same disk. When you save your work to disk, the computer uses the *filename* to identify the data and to keep the data for each file separate.

Naming Files with DOS

Every file on a single disk must have a separate name to distinguish it from other files on the same disk. The filename consists of a base name (up to eight characters) and an *extension* (up to three characters)—for example, CHAPTER9.MSW. The extension identifies the type of file (in this case **M**icro**s**oft **W**ord), and helps you group your files so you can enter commands that affect an entire group of files. For example, you can create a group of files with the filename extension .WK1 (for the memos you create in a given week). If you want to delete all those memos, enter a command to delete all the files with .WK1 as the extension. Common file extensions are listed in Table 3-1.

28

Saving Files on a Disk

When you begin typing information into your computer, the information is initially stored in RAM, the electronic storage facility. If you blow a fuse or accidentally turn off your computer, it's bye-bye document! To prevent such a loss of important information, your work in a more stable location—on a disk.

Since you've already created a file with a unique filename and entered information for that file, all you need to do to save the file to disk is press a key, usually one of the F (function) keys. The system automatically writes the electronic file from RAM to the magnetic disk.

When you save files to disk, you can store hundreds or thousands of files. It's great that disks can hold so much information, but it also results in a problem—keeping all these files organized.

Organizing Files on a Floppy Disk

Organizing files on a floppy disk is not all that difficult, because you normally don't store very many files per disk. Even if you store as many as 30 files on a single disk, you can manage to search through a list of files fairly quickly.

Table 3-1. *IBM File Extensions*

File Extension	File Type
.ASM	Assembly language program
.BAK	Backup file
.BAS	BASIC language program
.BAT	Batch file
.C	C language program
.COM	Command (program) file
.DAT	Data file
.DBF	dBASE file
.DOC	Document file
.EXE	Executable program file
.HLP	Help file
.NDX	dBASE index file
.OBJ	Object code file
.OVL	Overlay file
.PAS	Pascal language program
.TXT	Text (ASCII) file
.WKS, .WK1, WK2, WK3	Lotus 1-2-3 files
.WP	WordPerfect file
.WS	WordStar file

29

Even so, you should follow three standard procedures to make the information more accessible:

1. Give each file a unique name that helps you remember what's in the file. For example, LETTER.DOC is not a good filename.
2. Label each disk with the files stored on that disk and the date. That way, you'll know what's on the disk and which disk holds the most recent revisions.
3. Copy any files you don't use very often to separate disks, and erase the original files from the disks you use often. That way, you don't have a bunch of junk files to wade through when you're looking for something important.

Organizing Files on a Hard Disk

Organizing files on a hard disk is more of a challenge. Even a small hard disk can hold several hundred files. If you had to search through a list of a thousand files stored on your hard disk, it would take hours and be one of the most frustrating tasks you ever encountered.

To get around this problem, you need to create directories and subdirectories to help organize your files. A directory is like a filing cabinet. Just as you can have several filing cabinets in your office, you can have several directories on your hard disk. The subdirectories are like drawers in the filing cabinet that store a particular group of files.

The operating system has everything you need to set up directories. First activate the drive that you want to hold the directory. When the proper drive is active, tell the system to make a directory, and type the name of the directory. The operating system creates the directory, and it's ready to start accepting files.

30

Directories and subdirectories form a structure, shown in Figure 3-3, that looks like a family tree. At the root of this tree is the *root directory*, which usually holds your operating system (such as DOS, UNIX, or System 7.0). When you start up your computer, the first thing it does is look for system files in the root directory so it can orient itself. Out of the root directory sprouts the directories and subdirectories that make up the *directory tree*.

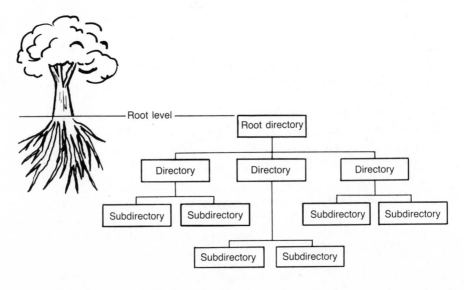

Figure 3-3.   A directory tree.

For example, I used a word processing program called WordStar to write this book. I stored my WordStar program files in a directory called WS4. All the chapters of this book are in a subdirectory called PC, which stands for Personal Computers. Each chapter is in a separate file—C1.WS, C2.WS, etc.

Whenever you want to use a particular file, you must tell your computer where to look for it. For example, if you want to run Word-Star, give your computer a map of where to look for the files. This map must include the disk drive and directory where the program files are located. If you stored the files in drive D, in the subdirectory WS4, you first need to tell your computer to activate drive D by typing **d:** and pressing the Enter key. Then, you need to tell your computer to change directories to the WS4 directory. Do this by typing the command **cd** (change directories) followed by a backslash (\) and the directory name, **ws4**. The entire command, **cd\ws4**, is called a *path*.

These paths can get long. For example, you may need to tell your computer to get the CUB file that's in subdirectory LION, in the directory ZOO, in drive C. The path would look like this:

`c:\zoo\lion\cub`

Figure 3-4 shows a schematic of how the disk drive uses the path above to locate the CUB file.

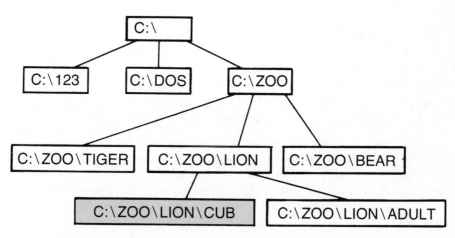

Figure 3-4.   A schematic of a directory path.

Once you get accustomed to using directories, they're pretty straightforward; just weave through your directory tree to your destination. Believe me, it's a lot easier and faster than swapping disks.

31

Performing Daily Tasks with the Operating System

You've already seen that the operating system is the overseer, the supervisor, of all your computer's activity. In addition to its managerial role, the operating system offers several features that help you manage the files you create.

Seeing What's on a Disk

You can use the operating system to find out what's stored on a particular disk. First, make sure that the drive that the disk is in is the active drive, then enter the command to list the contents of that drive and press the Enter key. For example, with DOS, type **dir** (directory) next to the prompt and press Enter. DOS then displays a list of files on the disk.

32

With a Macintosh computer, it's even easier. Just use the mouse to point to a picture of the disk that's displayed on screen, and press the mouse button twice in quick succession. This is called double-clicking.

Insuring Your Work

You may have heard horror stories about people losing vast amounts of information that they entered into their computers. Don't let these stories scare you off. Most of these people lost information only because they failed to take the steps necessary to protect it.

Your operating system offers everything you need to protect your valuable work. If you buy an applications program, you can copy the disks that came with the software package so you'll have a backup in case anything happens to the originals. You can also copy individual files from one disk to another to protect against accidental erasure or faulty disks.

The DOS copy command is pretty flexible. You can use it to copy an individual file or group of files. You can even copy a group of files that you created on a given day. The copy commands are very easy to execute; the few minutes you spend backing up your work each day or each week are well worth it.

Performing Housekeeping Tasks

After you've worked with your computer for a while, you'll find that you have vast amounts of information stored in one place or another, and you probably have several versions of the same documents and reports. Eventually, you'll need to get rid of some of the clutter.

With the operating system, you can erase a file or a group of files, remove directories (after you erase all files in the directory), and perform any other required housekeeping tasks.

Restoring Files

When you erase a file from a floppy or hard disk (on purpose or by mistake), your computer doesn't physically erase the file. Instead, your computer leaves the file completely intact on the disk. If you try to load the file or view the file in a directory listing, your computer pretends it's not there.

Because your computer pretends that an erased file does not exist, utility programs can "unerase" previously erased files, but only as long as you have not saved or modified another file to that same disk. When you save or modify a file, it may take up the space previously occupied by the file you accidentally erased.

When you erase a file by mistake, don't save or modify any files on that disk. Get a utility program (Norton Utilities, PC Tools Deluxe, MacTools Deluxe) and "unerase" your file. Once you have "unerased" a file, you can treat the file normally.

Checking Disks

You can use the operating system to check the free space remaining on a particular disk. If you just created a document consisting of about 2,000 bytes or characters and you want to store it on a disk that already has several files on it, you can have the operating system check the disk to make sure that there's enough room for the new file.

Before you can add or modify any files on a disk, you need to make sure that the disk has enough empty space. If you are using an IBM or compatible computer, you're probably using an operating system called MS-DOS, PC DOS, or just plain DOS. To check the amount of free space on a disk using MS-DOS, type DIR and press the Return key.

33

MS-DOS displays a list of files on the disk including the file extension, date and time the file was created or last modified, and the size of the file. At the end of this directory listing, MS-DOS lists the total number of files on the disk and the amount of free space remaining, measured in bytes:

```
C:\GSdir

Volume in drive C is DOS400
Volume Serial Number is 0f17-18E4
Directory of C:\GS

.              <DIR>      02-24-90   11:40a
..             <DIR>      02-24-90   11:40a
READ    ME       3441  04-20-88    4:44p
CAT1           227723  04-20-88    4:44p
GS      COM      3432  04-20-88    4:44p
START   EXE     77871  04-20-88    4:44p
ROSTER  FIL       936  03-19-90    7:23a
ROSTER  SAV       936  04-20-88    4:44p
CAT2           129649  04-20-88    4:44p
EGAME   EXE     62375  04-20-88    4:44p
TITLE   EXE     17133  05-02-88    3:29p
        11 File(s)      638976 bytes free

C:\GS
```

For Macintosh users, just look in the upper-right corner of each disk window. The window tells you how much space is already taken by existing files and how much free space remains, measured in kilobytes (see Figure 3-5).

Keeping Track of Time

To let you know when you created or modified a file, the operating system keeps track of the date and time. Some computers have a battery-powered clock inside that works even after you turn off the computer. With other computers, the operating system asks you to enter the date and time when you start it up.

After you type the new date or time, the operating system retains this date or time until you change it or turn off your computer. Many applications programs automatically insert the date and time from your

34

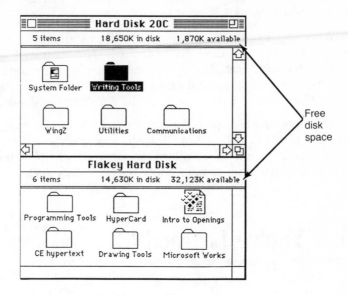

Figure 3-5. *Viewing free disk space on a Macintosh computer.*

computer into the documents you create. For example, if you're writing a business letter, you can tell the program to insert the date, saving you the time of typing it in.

Giving Your Operating System a Friendly Face

Computers expect you to know what you're doing. On IBM and compatible computers, the DOS prompt may appear on a blank screen, almost daring you to do something useful. Unless you know what to type, you can't go on.

To solve this problem, you can buy *graphical user interface (GUI)* programs, which make the operating system easier to use. Rather than having to type cryptic commands on a clueless screen, you can choose commands and files from menus, as you can with the Macintosh. Micro-

35

soft Windows, a popular GUI program, can protect you from the intimidation caused by a blank screen.

With a GUI program, the detailed information about a file, such as its size or the date and time it was created, remains out of sight, making the screen less cluttered. This setup also makes it easier to run programs. You don't have to worry about making typos when you're entering a command; just use the mouse to point to the command and select it.

Some popular GUI programs available for IBM and compatible computers include DeskMate, GEM Desktop, and Microsoft Windows. These programs usually come with additional *utilities*, or office tools, such as calendars or calculators to help you with your daily tasks.

What You've Learned

36

Like any good manager, the operating system is fairly invisible, usually working behind the scenes to make sure everything runs smoothly, and preparing the way for the applications programs. Before you move on to the individual applications programs, review the basics of what you learned here:

- ► Before you can use your computer, you must start it up with an operating system.
- ► There are two types of operating systems: some lead you with prompts, some with menus.
- ► You can view the contents of a disk by telling your operating system to display a directory.
- ► Before you can store anything on a new disk, you must format the disk.
- ► After you start up your computer, you can run an applications program that helps you perform specific tasks.
- ► Each of your creations is stored in a file on a disk. To work with the file you must retrieve it from disk.
- ► The operating system lets you copy files and disks to protect your work.
- ► You can use the operating system to set up the directories and subdirectories on your hard disk.
- ► Graphical user interface (GUI) programs make your operating system easier to use.

Chapter 4

Introduction to Software

In This Chapter

- ▶ *What you need to know when you're shopping*
  for software
- ▶ *What to expect when you open a software package*
- ▶ *Using reference cards and keyboard templates*
  to make your job easier
- ▶ *Getting help from software companies*
- ▶ *Understanding program upgrades*

If you don't have a computer yet, the best way to shop for one is to work backward. Figure out what type of software you want to use, then purchase everything you need to work with that software. As Table 4-1 shows, there's a software program that can help you do just about any job you can think of. We'll talk about each of these in a separate chapter of this book.

Table 4-1. *Software Programs*

Program Type	Purpose
Word processor	Writing letters and reports, composing books, writing articles
Database	Storing and manipulating information, analyzing data entered into the system, generating client reports, printing mailing labels
Spreadsheet	Balancing accounts, keeping track of schedules, tracking materials, estimating job costs, determining averages, automating quality control
Desktop publishing	Printing newsletters, creating flyers, printing menus
Telecommunications	Sending/receiving data from another computer
Graphics	Creating graphs, generating mechanical drawings, illustrating manuals, computer-aided design (CAD), computer-aided engineering (CAE)
Programming languages	Writing your own programs, creating your own software applications, customizing commericial software to your own needs

> ▶ **Tip:** The key to choosing the right software is to know what you want the computer to do. This book is an excellent start. Another big help is to talk to people you know who use computers for the same type of work. Call associates, colleagues, competitors, friends, and sales people. Ask them what system they use, what they like about it, and what they dislike.

Beginner or Advanced?

Before buying a program, decide how important it will be to you. A writer wants the best word processor possible, but might only want a spreadsheet that's simple enough to learn and use without fancy features to worry about.

For programs that you will use for your job or business, get the most advanced possible. Table 4-2 lists some of the more popular advanced programs for different software categories:

Table 4-2. Advanced Software Programs

Software Type	Program Name
Word processor	WordPerfect, Microsoft Word, FullWrite Professional
Spreadsheet	Lotus 1-2-3, Microsoft Excel, Quattro Pro, WingZ
Database	dBASE III Plus, dBASE IV, Paradox, 4th Dimension, FoxBase
Graphics	Harvard Presentation Graphics, Lotus Freelance Plus

39

These advanced programs are expensive and more difficult to learn because they offer so many features. However, once you know how to use the program, these features make your job much easier, whether it's writing, balancing budgets, financial forecasting, or drawing blueprints.

For programs that are not as important to your job or work, you can save money and time by buying a beginner's program instead. Table 4-3 lists several popular beginner programs:

Table 4-3. Beginner Software Programs

Software Type	Program Name
Word processor	Professional Write, Q&A Write, Write Now, PC-Write
Spreadsheet	Professional Plan, AsEasyAs, MacCalc, PC-Calc
Database	Q&A, Reflex, FileMaker Pro, PC-File
Graphics	PFS: First Graphics, VP-Graphics, MacPaint, MacDraw

40 Can Your Computer Run the Program?

Remember, before you buy any software package, make sure your computer and operating system can run it. The *minimum hardware requirements* are printed on the outside of every software package. If the software requirements specify that you need an IBM or compatible computer but you own a Macintosh, then you can't use the software with your equipment. Here is a summary of some requirements for programs:

Computer Type (IBM, Macintosh, Apple II). This describes the type of computer needed to run the program.

Memory (required and recommended). The *required* memory lists the minimum amount of random access memory (RAM) needed to run this program. If your computer has less RAM, then you cannot use the program. The *recommended* memory lists the minimum amount of memory needed to run the program effectively. If you have less than the recommended memory, the program may run slowly, or you may not be able to use all the features that the program offers.

Operating System (type and version number). To run any program, your computer must use the right type of operating system, such as DOS, UNIX, or OS/2. Your operating system must also be the right version, such as DOS 3.0 or higher.

Monitors (color or monochrome). Some programs require color monitors that can display graphics. Because IBM and compatible computers can use several different types of color monitors, a program may only work on a specific type. If a program needs a color monitor but you only have a monochrome monitor, you may not be able to run the program, or you may not be able to use all the features that the program offers. (See VGA and CGA in Chapter 8.)

Hard Disk (required or recommended). If a program requires a hard disk, you cannot use the program without one. If a program recommends that you use a hard disk, you should use one to get your money's worth out of the program. Otherwise, you're going to get very tired of swapping disks.

What to Expect from a Software Package

41

Applications programs usually include a user's manual, a reference manual, floppy disks, and a registration card.

Instruction Manuals

User's manuals have a Getting Started section that tells you how to copy the program on your computer, how to get the program up and running, and how to use the program by function. Reference manuals list all program commands and their functions alphabetically.

The quality of these manuals varies from package to package —some software companies just don't invest a lot of time and effort into developing high-quality documentation.

Even when software companies do invest in their documentation, the manuals are nearly always incomplete. Many publishers print the manuals while the program is still being perfected, so they can beat their competitors to market. In the meantime, the programmers keep improving the program and adding features not included in the manuals.

As a result, nearly all programs have hidden features. To explain how these hidden features work, publishers may include additional instructions on a floppy disk, usually in a file called README. You can then load the floppy disk into your computer and display the additional instructions on screen or print them out and insert them in one of your manuals.

Floppy Disks

The applications program consists of several program files stored on one or more floppy disks. Remember, before you buy a program, make sure it comes with the type and size of floppy disks that your computer can use. Table 4-4 shows the more popular computers and the type and size of disks that they can handle.

Table 4-4. *Disk Types and Sizes*

Computer	Disk Type	Disk Capacity	Disk Size
Macintosh	Double-density	800K	3½″
Macintosh	High-density	1.44M	3½″
IBM	Double-density	360K	5¼″
IBM	Double-density	720K	3½″
IBM	High-density	1.2M	5¼″
IBM	High-density	1.44M	3½″

42

Some software for the IBM may contain only one size disk: *either* 3 1/2-inch *or* 5 1/4-inch. If the disks included do not fit your computer, then you have to send in a coupon requesting an exchange. Other packages get around this problem by including both sizes of disks. The disk size should be written on the outside of the box.

Registration Card

Every program comes with a registration card that you must mail back to the publisher. This card lets the publisher know who owns a legal copy of the program.

Software companies offer several perks for sending in the card. They will answer your questions over the phone, send free newsletters describing tips for using the program, and offer program *upgrades* at greatly reduced prices. As soon as you open your software package, fill out the card and send it in.

> **Tip:** Version 1.0 is the first version of a program. Version 1.1 or 1.5 is the same program with minor improvements, Version 2.0 is the same program with a major improvement, and so on. If you already own an older version of a program, you can buy the newer version at a greatly reduced price. Typical upgrade charges range between $10 and $150. To take advantage of this price break, however, you must have sent in the registration card from the older version of the program. Some companies may even require you to trade in the older version.

Reference Cards and Templates

All programs assign commands to specific keys or to combinations of keys on the keyboard. Because it may take a while for you to memorize the commands, many programs include reference cards or keyboard templates.

43

Reference cards list the program commands and the corresponding keys. You can keep the card next to your keyboard and glance at the card whenever you need help.

Keyboard templates lie on top of your keyboard and usually wrap around the function keys. Printed next to each function key or commonly used command key is the command or function that the key performs.

> **Tip:** Remember, before you actually begin using an application program, copy the program to your hard disk or to another set of floppy disks, and put the original disks in a safe place. Use the copies, rather than the originals, for your daily work. If something happens to the copies, you still have the originals to fall back on.

Write-Protecting the Disks

Normally, a computer can add or delete information from a floppy disk. However, if you've just paid $800 for a software program, you probably don't want to change any of it. So before you do anything, *write-protect* the disks. Write protection lets your computer read information from the disk, but prevents the computer from doing anything to that information.

As you saw in Figure 2-3, the 5 1/4-inch disks have a square notch cut in the corner. To write-protect these disks, cover the notch with a write-protect sticker. The 3 1/2-inch disks have a sliding write-protect tab. Slide the tab so that you can see through the window, and the disk is write-protected.

44

 Note: Write-protecting your disks also protects your investment from viruses, as you'll see later.

One of the manuals that came with your software should tell you how to copy the disks. If it doesn't, refer to the manual that came with your operating system.

Using Software

The computer is a very literal beast—it understands only what you tell it. So you need to know how to talk to your computer, what keys to press. To help you put the commands in some sort of context, the following list introduces the most basic tasks that every application program performs:

▶ Running the program
▶ Creating a file
▶ Saving a file
▶ Entering data
▶ Editing data
▶ Printing data
▶ Quitting the program

Running the Program

Running the program means starting it up—getting yourself a screen on which you can actually start doing your work. The first step to running a program consists of making the program files available to your computer, that is, putting the disk that holds the program files into your computer's disk drive, and making sure the computer knows what drive it's in. The following list describes what you must do in three of the more common situations:

> *IBM (or IBM compatible, using floppy disks).* Load your startup disk in drive A, and make sure `A:>` or `A>` is displayed on screen.
>
> *Macintosh (or other menu-driven system, using floppy disks).* Load the startup disk in drive A. Use the mouse to point to the icon representing the program disk and press the mouse button, activating the drive.
>
> *IBM (or IBM compatible using a hard disk).* Make sure the directory to which you copied your program files is active. This consists of telling your computer to activate a particular disk drive and then giving the computer a path to the directory. For example, if you copied the program files for WordStar 4.0 to drive D of your hard disk and in a directory called WS4, first make sure `D>` is displayed on screen, then type **cd\ws4**, telling your computer to "change directory to WS4," and press Enter. Your computer would then display `D:\WS4>`, indicating that the directory is now active.

45

Once your computer knows where the program files are located, enter the command to run the startup program. You can enter this command in either of two ways: choose the command from a menu, or enter the command at the prompt.

If you have a Macintosh or similar menu-driven system, just choose the Open command from one of the menus, or use the mouse to point to the program icon, and double-click on the icon.

To start most programs on an IBM or clone, you need to type a command at the prompt. The command is usually an acronym or abbreviation of the program's name. The user's manuals tell you what you need to type. If you don't have the manual handy, type **dir *.exe** or **dir *.com** at the prompt and press Enter. Your computer displays a list of program files that are on the disk, as shown in Figure 4-1.

```
C:\WP51>dir *.exe

 Volume in drive C has no label
 Volume Serial Number is 077B-10E3
 Directory of  C:\WP51

INSTALL  EXE     54272 01-19-90   12:00p
CONVERT  EXE    109049 01-19-90   12:00p
GRAPHCNV EXE    111104 01-19-90   12:00p
MACROCNV EXE     24508 01-19-90   12:00p
WPINFO   EXE      8704 01-19-90   12:00p
SPELL    EXE     55808 01-19-90   12:00p
NWPSETUP EXE     28672 01-19-90   12:00p
WP       EXE    220672 01-19-90   12:00p
        8 File(s)    8552448 bytes free

C:\WP51>
```

46

Figure 4-1. A directory listing of program files on a disk.

This list gives you some ideas for commands you might try, such as WP for WordPerfect. Table 4-5 shows several commands for popular IBM programs.

Table 4-5. Startup Commands for Popular IBM Programs

Startup Command	Program
DBASE	dBASE III Plus
123	Lotus 1-2-3
WP	WordPerfect
GWBASIC	GW-BASIC
TURBO	Turbo Pascal
TC	Turbo C
WORD	Microsoft Word
EXCEL	Microsoft Excel
PW	Professional Write
FIRST	PFS: First Choice
FP	PFS: First Publisher
Q	Quattro Professional

After you enter the command for running the program, it takes a while for the computer to read the program disk and load the program into RAM. When it's done, it displays an *opening screen* that usually contains the *main menu* listing several of the commands you may want to use to begin. An example of such a screen is shown in Figure 4-2.

Main menu

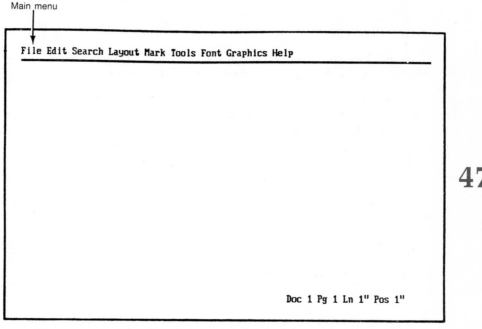

File Edit Search Layout Mark Tools Font Graphics Help

Doc 1 Pg 1 Ln 1" Pos 1"

Figure 4-2. WordPerfect's opening screen.

47

For example, the screen may list commands for creating a new file, opening an old file, renaming a file, and so on. You may also see a menu bar at the top or bottom of the screen. This menu bar contains several *pull-down* menus for specific sets of commands. To pull down a menu and view its contents, simply press the key associated with that menu or use the mouse to click open the menu.

Entering Data

In Chapter 3, you learned how to create, name, and save a file.

> ▶ **Tip:** It's good practice to save your work often—every ten to fifteen minutes. That way, if the power suddenly fails (even for only a second) you won't lose too much work. And if you make a big mistake, you can go back to the previous version and start over.

Opening a file consists of getting information that's already stored on disk and displaying it on screen so you can work with it.

Just as with running a program, you can't retrieve information from a disk until the disk is loaded into your computer and the drive or directory that contains the files is active. Once that's done, just enter the command for opening the file, and tell your computer the name of the file to open.

48

On a Macintosh, simply double-click on the disk icon to activate the drive and to view a directory of files on the disk, then double-click on the file you want to open.

With most IBM programs, you need to enter a command to open the file. This command varies from program to program, but is usually displayed on screen to help you remember. Table 4-6 lists the commands used for opening files in several popular programs.

Table 4-6. Open File Commands

Open File Command	Program
Type **use** and then the name of the file	dBASE III Plus
Press F5	WordPerfect
Type **d**	WordStar
Press / F L	Lotus 1-2-3

Editing Data

Now that your work is displayed on screen, you can edit it and play with it as much as you want. Because your work is stored electronically in RAM, making changes is simple. Adding, deleting, or moving information is nothing more than an electronic version of cut-and-paste. For instance, if you write a concluding paragraph and then decide that it would make an excellent introduction, just lift the paragraph from the end and move it to the beginning. If your inventory records don't balance against the actual count, go back and check the figures you entered. If a single number is wrong, change only that number and tell your computer to recalculate the total.

You'll find the editing feature to be the biggest time-saver associated with computers, and one of the most fun.

Printing Data

After you've perfected your file and stored it safely to disk, you can print the contents of your file on paper. If you used to use a typewriter to print your letters, you'll find that the computer printer is a lot more flexible. Depending on your printer and on your program, you can perform some of the following tricks:

49

► Print a list of names and addresses organized alphabetically, by ZIP code, by state, or by any other criteria you wish
► Print in different type styles, such as bold or italics
► Vary the size of print to set off areas of a form or report
► Print mailing labels
► Merge a form letter with a database that contains information about several customers to print out a series of personalized letters
► Vary print speed from draft mode to near letter quality mode.
► Vary the quality of the print from compressed to expanded.

Quitting a Program

When you've finished working with a particular program, you can quit the program, return to the operating system, and load another applications program. Common commands to quit a program include typing the words, **quit**, **exit**, or **system** and then pressing the Enter key, or simply pressing the Esc (Escape) key. One of the menus on screen usually tells you what to do to quit a program.

Special Program Features

Besides giving you the ability to run a program, save, edit, and print data, applications programs offer additional features to make the program easier to learn and use. They may also offer special features such as a calendar, alarm clock, or calculator to make such tools more convenient.

Tutorials

To help you start using the program immediately, many programs offer tutorials that let you practice with the program using imaginary data. If you make a mistake with imaginary data, you won't be as upset as if you make a mistake with your own important data.

50

The tutorial may be stored on disk or written in one of the manuals. If it's stored on disk, it's in a separate file that you can open; the User's manual should tell you the name of the file. Once you open the file, you can begin using the program on the imaginary data. If the tutorial is written in one of the manuals, you have to do some typing first; the User's manual tells you just what you need to type.

> **Tip:** For those of you who like to watch someone else work with a program before you try it, some software packages now include videotapes explaining how to use the program. Not something you want to save for a Friday night, but they do help.

Getting Help

When you're using a program and you get in a jam, it can be a real hassle to page through a book to find the answer, especially if the book has no index. Some programs offer help menus or help indexes to provide immediate help, as shown in Figure 4-3. Just open the menu or index to view a list of commands and what they do. To get more information about one of the items on the list, simply select the item, and the program displays additional information about that command.

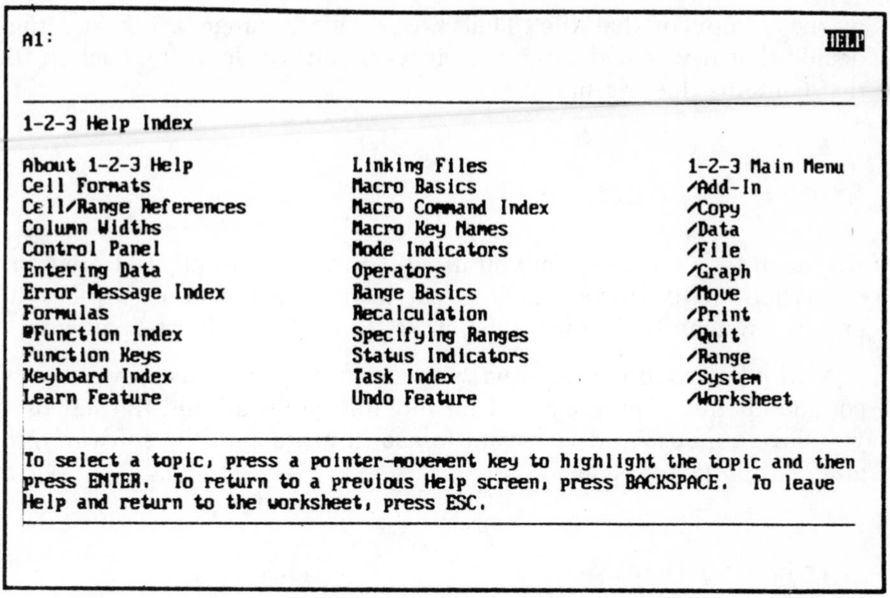

```
A1:                                                               HELP

─────────────────────────────────────────────────────────────────────
1-2-3 Help Index

About 1-2-3 Help         Linking Files          1-2-3 Main Menu
Cell Formats             Macro Basics           /Add-In
Cell/Range References    Macro Command Index    /Copy
Column Widths            Macro Key Names        /Data
Control Panel            Mode Indicators        /File
Entering Data            Operators              /Graph
Error Message Index      Range Basics           /Move
Formulas                 Recalculation          /Print
#Function Index          Specifying Ranges      /Quit
Function Keys            Status Indicators      /Range
Keyboard Index           Task Index             /System
Learn Feature            Undo Feature           /Worksheet

─────────────────────────────────────────────────────────────────────
To select a topic, press a pointer-movement key to highlight the topic and then
press ENTER.  To return to a previous Help screen, press BACKSPACE.  To leave
Help and return to the worksheet, press ESC.
─────────────────────────────────────────────────────────────────────
```

Figure 4-3.   The help index screen from Lotus 1-2-3.

51

Although this process is a lot easier than searching through a book, it can get very tiresome, especially if you're not sure what you want to do. To get around this problem, several programs offer *context-sensitive* help screens that explain commands for operations you may want to perform at a given time.

For example, if you try to print a file and your computer displays an error message saying

PRINTER NOT READY

you could open a context-sensitive help screen that would list possible solutions to your problem. When you get one of these error messages, you don't want to wade through commands you care nothing about; you just want to know what to do to fix the problem. Context-sensitive help screens do just that.

Backup Files

Many programs create backup files as insurance against mistakes. When you run the program and load a file, the program immediately makes a copy of that file. That way, if you change a file and then decide that it was better the way it was, you can load the backup file that contains the original.

Mouse Support

All Macintosh programs let you use a mouse, but not all IBM programs do. When an IBM program does use a mouse, it usually works with only a few brands of software such as IBM, Microsoft, or Logitech.

Mouse support means that you can use your mouse for choosing commands in the program and for moving things around the screen. If you have a mouse and you want to use it, make sure the software program supports a mouse.

52 Sharing Files

Different applications programs use different formats to handle the information that you enter. For example, WordStar uses a different format from WordPerfect. So if you try to use information that was created in one format with another format, you get all sorts of strange-looking symbols on your screen.

If you're in a business that requires you to share information with others, make sure that you have some way of converting what you receive or send into a usable form. There are a few software programs that are entirely devoted to this task, such as Software Bridge and Soft-Scan, that can convert several formats. Some word processing and database programs also offer less comprehensive conversion features. You should check to make sure they meet your needs.

Unfortunately, not all programs offer a conversion feature. In such cases, you can share data by storing the files in a universal format such as ASCII (pronounced ASK-ee), which stands for American Standard Code for Information Interchange. This conversion is not the most ideal; you lose a lot in the translation, such as special codes that lay out your information just as you wanted it. All that gets translated is the meaning, the text. Hence, these ASCII files are often referred to as text files.

Most programs offer some way to convert your files to the ASCII format. Some programs offer a Save As command that lets you save the file either in the ASCII format or in the format of the program you're using. It's a good idea to save the file once in your program's format and then save it again under another name in the ASCII format. That way, at least the original version retains the special codes you used to lay it out. If your program does not offer the Save As feature, then it may let you print the file to a disk instead of to your printer. Sometimes you can even use this Print-to-Disk feature to convert your file to ASCII *and* retain the special codes.

Menus and Shortcuts

You've already seen how menus work to save you the trouble of memorizing and typing a command every time you need it. Most current programs use at least a few menus, if only to serve as helpful reminders.

The only problem with menus is that once you know what you're doing, they can really slow you down and they take up a lot of space on your screen. That doesn't mean that you'll just have to live with it. Programmers realized the drawbacks and have worked around them with two features that help wean you from menus.

53

The first feature lets you simply turn off the menu and enter the commands directly. The second feature lets you use shortcut keys to perform a task that you would otherwise have to choose from a menu. For example, a program might have a menu called Edit that has a list of edit tasks, including one for deleting a word. To delete a word, you need to move the cursor to the word, press one key to open the Edit menu, then press another key to choose the Delete command from the menu. To let you bypass the menu, the program may offer a shortcut key; you simply move the cursor to the word you want to delete, hold down one key, press another, and bingo, the word is gone.

Dialog Boxes

Programs may display windows, called *dialog boxes*, on screen asking for your input before carrying out a command you've just given. Sometimes they contain options for you to choose from, other times they have a space for you to enter information, and occasionally they warn you about something that's about to happen—to doublecheck that you know what you're doing.

For example, the dialog box in Figure 4-4 would appear if you were using Microsoft Word on your Macintosh and had chosen the Open command from the file menu. With this window, you would choose the file you want from the list of all files in the active drive, saving you the bother of remembering the actual file name.

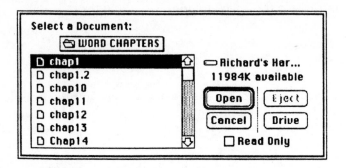

54

Figure 4-4.   A dialog box.

If a dialog box lists several options, you need to choose one before continuing. These options are usually displayed with *check boxes* and *radio buttons*. The radio buttons put the dialog box in a certain mode. For example, a dialog box may appear that asks if you want to save a document. At the bottom of the box may be two buttons, one that says Save As Is and one that says ASCII. By pressing one or the other of the buttons, you're not telling the program to do anything yet; you're just telling it that when it does save the file, save it in a particular format. The check boxes (for example a box that says OK or SAVE) are what you use to actually execute the command.

When Something Goes Wrong

Occasionally, you'll be using a program when suddenly everything stops working. The program and data may still appear on the screen, but you can't do anything. No matter what key you press, no matter what command you try to enter, the program just won't budge. Even after waiting several minutes, the computer has the same blank stare.

When this happens, you've experienced a *crash*. All the data that was in RAM—that is, any data that you entered since the last time you saved your work—is lost. Crashes don't occur very often, but if you don't save your work and make backups of your files, a crash can be devastating.

A computer crash occurs for a variety of reasons, none predictable. Sometimes you may press certain keys at exactly the wrong time. Other times your computer may crash if you are running two or more programs at the same time, either through using multitasking software such as OS/2, or programs that temporarily pop up from memory (memory-resident programs, like Sidekick or Prokey).

A crash does not physically damage your computer or disks, but it does prevent you from saving any data you created since the last time you saved your file. So if you save a file, type five more pages, and your computer suddenly crashes, you lose the past five pages you've written.

To recover from a crash, turn your computer off, wait approximately ten seconds, and turn it back on again. With some computers you can press a reset button instead. For IBM and compatible computers, you can *reboot* your computer with your operating system. Rebooting is simply a process of restarting your computer. To reboot using DOS, make sure the DOS disk is in one of your drives, then hold down the Ctrl (Control) key, hold down the Alt key, and press the Del key.

55

What You've Learned

In this chapter, you learned most of the basics about applications programs. If you get a program that's menu-driven and offers plenty of context-sensitive help, you probably know enough from reading this chapter to get started using the program. You may not be able to do the fancy stuff, but at least you can get going.

In the next few chapters, you'll get to see some more detail about specific types of applications programs. But for now, let's go over what you learned here:

▶ When you're shopping for an applications program, figure out what you want the program to do, and then talk to people about the programs they use.

▶ Make sure your equipment can run the software program.

▶ Every software package contains manuals, a registration card, and one or more floppy disks.

▶ Reference cards and keyboard templates help you remember commands when you're starting out.

▶ Program upgrades are improved versions of the program.

▶ To find out about the hidden features that are not documented in the User's manual, look for a file called README.

▶ ASCII files let you share data between different programs and computers.

▶ Enter commands either by typing the command or by choosing it from a menu.

▶ A context-sensitive help feature gives you immediate help for whatever you're working on.

▶ Conversion programs let you share files that were created in a different format.

56

▶ To recover from a computer crash, you must restart your computer.

Chapter 5

Word Processing

In This Chapter

▶ *Mastering the electronic document*

▶ *Using the computer to proofread your work*

▶ *A thesaurus at your fingertips*

▶ *Molding the page*

▶ *Automatic page numbering*

▶ *Simplified outlining and indexing*

▶ *Merging information from a database with a form letter*

▶ *Choosing between different word processors*

The word processor is essentially a fancy typewriter that not only makes typing a lot easier, but can actually help you compose and perfect your work. It has an endless supply of electronic paper that scrolls past the screen as you type, and because it's electronic, you don't have to worry about making mistakes. Just go back and type over the errors—no messy white-out, no erasing, and best of all, no retyping.

Your computer proofreads your work at your command, and even offers suggestions to help you with spelling. Once you find the errors, correcting them is easy. Delete the mistake and type the correction. Because it's so easy, you can experiment and mold your language into the perfect sculpture.

When you've finished, send the finished document from your computer to your printer, and watch the perfect copy come out—clean and sharp.

Controlling the Electronic Document

Although word processing programs vary in complexity and in the number of features they offer, you must perform the same four basic steps when working with any of these programs:

58

Type. You need to type the first draft of whatever you're working on or at least a portion of it.

Edit. Once you have something to work with, you can play with the information on screen until it is just as you want it.

Format. When you have finalized the content and ironed out the wrinkles, you can begin working on the appearance of the document. This includes setting margins and line spacing, adding headings, and changing typestyles.

Print. You finally get to see the document on paper. You also can enter commands to change the typestyle of the entire document, merge two documents, and insert graphs and tables from one document into another.

Creating a Document

Remember, the first thing you need to do when you start working with any software program is open a file. When you open a file for a word processing program, the screen is fairly empty. There may be a menu or a menu bar displayed, but other than that, it's not much to look at.

To begin creating a document, simply type as you would on a typewriter; the cursor moves from left to right across the screen, leaving characters in its wake.

Wordwrapping

If you're used to working with a typewriter, you may tend to hit the Return key at the end of every line. Don't. The word processor does it for you. When the cursor reaches the end of the line, it automatically jumps to the next line, *wrapping* the words from one line to the next, as shown in Figure 5-1. Hitting Return can throw off the wordwrap feature. Use the Return only at the end of a paragraph or in other cases where you want to end a line.

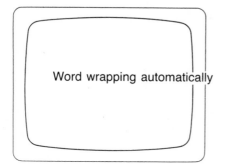 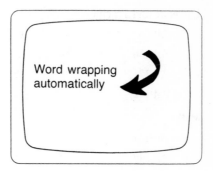

59

Figure 5-1. Wordwrapping automatically adjusts text to fit within the left and right margins.

Foreign Language and Scientific Symbols

If you need to write scientific papers or in a foreign language, you must have a system with the required symbols.

Although some word processors are designed especially for such uses, most word processing programs can handle only the common symbols. In WordPerfect and in many other word processing programs, for example, you can hold down the Alt (Alternative) key and type a three-digit number for the symbol you want to type. (You must type the number on the numeric pad, *not* on the usual number keys.) Table 5-1 shows only a few of the many symbols available.

Table 5-1. Alt-Key Combinations for Special Symbols in WordPerfect

Alt-key Combination	Special Symbol
Foreign Languages	
Alt-128	Ç
Alt-133	à
Alt-148	ö
Alt-168	¿
Currency and Fractions	
Alt-155	¢
Alt-156	£
Alt-171	½
Alt-172	¼
Math	
Alt-241	±
Alt-242	≥
Alt-243	≤
Alt-246	÷
Alt-251	√
Line Drawing	
Alt-179	│
Alt-183	┐
Alt-187	╗
Alt-191	┐
Alt-203	╦
Alt-205	═
Alt-207	╧

Editing the Document

Once you have some text on screen, start moving around the screen and entering changes. How fast you can move and what editing options you have depend on your equipment and experience, but all word processing programs offer some basic tools to get you started.

> ▶ **Tip:** Remember, you can move the cursor anywhere within the document by using the arrow keys on your keyboard or by using a mouse. You can move to the beginning of the screen with the Home key or to the end with the End key. Press PgUp (Page Up) to see the previous screen or PgDn (Page Down) to see the next screen. Most word processing programs offer combination keys that let you move the cursor from word to word, to the beginning or end of a line or paragraph, or even to a specific page.

Insert or Overstrike?

You can type corrections in either of two *modes* (ways): *Insert* or *Overstrike*. In Insert mode, the cursor inserts characters into the document without deleting any characters. If you want to insert a word between two words, move the cursor between the two words and type the addition; the surrounding words shift to make room. In Overstrike mode, you type over what's already on screen. If you want to replace one word with another, just type over the word you want to delete.

> ⊘ **Warning:** If you're used to working on a typewriter and using the Backspace key to move back to a word, don't try it on the word processor. The Backspace key moves the cursor back, but it erases every character on its way.

Most programs start in the Insert mode because it's the safest. To change from Insert to Overstrike and vice versa, press the Ins (Insert) key.

> ▶ **Note:** When a program starts in a certain mode, that mode is referred to as the *default* mode. Because nothing was specified, the program defaults to a particular setting. The default mode is usually the safest or most common option. Many programs let you change default settings to the settings you most commonly use.

62 *Deleting Characters, Words, and Lines*

The simplest way to delete characters on screen is to move the cursor to the character you want to delete and press the Del (Delete) key. This key works a little differently from program to program; sometimes the cursor deletes the character it's on; other times it deletes the character to the right. In either case, you'll get used to it pretty quickly.

Although the Del key is about the safest key you can use to delete characters, it's also the slowest. Most programs offer ways to delete larger chunks of text, such as words, lines, paragraphs, or entire sections. The keys used to perform these deletions vary from program to program.

Automatic Rewrapping

As you type corrections, add or delete words, and insert phrases into your document, you'll notice that you don't have to worry about adjusting the surrounding text to accommodate the change. The word processor does it automatically, rearranging the words in the entire document to compensate for whatever change you enter.

Working with Blocks

Usually, revising a document is not a simple matter of changing a word here or there or correcting typos. When you need to delete an entire sentence or even rearrange the paragraphs to present your points in a more logical flow, most word processing programs offer *block commands*. Using these commands is a simple two-step process:

1. Mark or select the block you want to work with.
2. Enter a command, telling the program what to do with the block.

For example, if you want to move a block, enter a command at the beginning and end of the block you want to move. The program highlights the entire block, showing you what you've just marked. Move the cursor to the place where you want to move the block, and enter the command for moving a block. The word processor moves the block from the old position to the new one and rearranges the text to accommodate the change. The following list summarizes common block commands:

63

Move takes a block of text from one place to another.

Cut deletes an entire block of text. In some programs, the block *retires* to a holding area so you can get it back if you make a mistake. Be careful, though, most of these holding cells hold only one block at a time. When you send another block there, it writes over the previous block.

Paste takes a block from a holding area and inserts it back into the text.

Copy keeps the block in its original location and copies the block into another location.

Change Line Spacing adjusts the amount of space around and within a paragraph. It's good for those chunks of type you want to set off from the rest of the text.

Undoing Your Changes

When you start seeing how much you can do with block commands, you may worry that you can do an equal amount of damage to your document. The biggest protection you have against unintentional changes is the document you saved to disk.

For minor mistakes, such as deleting a line or a paragraph, most programs have a safety buffer, a lot like the holding area mentioned above. If you unintentionally erase some text, you can usually get it back by entering an "Undo" command.

Search and Replace

When Margaret Mitchell wrote *Gone With The Wind*, she named her heroine Pansy O'Hara, but at the last minute changed her mind. Some poor editor got the job of searching for *Pansy* on nearly every page of the book and replacing it with *Scarlett*.

To help you in such cases, word processors offer a search and replace feature that searches an entire document for whatever letter, number, word, or phrase you want and replaces it with the new text you specify. You can even have the word processor wait for your final OK before replacing

64

To use this feature, move the cursor to the place in the document where you want the search to start, and enter the search command. The program asks you what you want to search for and what is the replacement. You specify whether you want the word processor to wait for your OK. Then unleash search and replace and watch it go.

Spell Checking

It's always good to have another set of eyes look over a letter or manuscript before you send it out. Many word processors include dictionaries of various sizes that can check your document for spelling errors, typos, repeated words (such as the the), and incorrect capitalization (tHe).

If a spell checking program finds a word that doesn't match, it stops and waits for you to enter a correction or give your OK. These programs may even offer suggestions for correct spellings. If the word is OK, and you don't want the spell checker to stop on the same word again, you can enter the word into the program's dictionary or into your own personal dictionary.

A spell checking program is just that. It does not determine whether you have used the right word, just whether the word is spelled correctly. If you type **in** when you mean to type **on** the word processor passes over it.

Choosing the Right Word

If you can't think of the right word, press a button to open the thesaurus. Enter the best word you can come up with, and your word processor will display a list of synonyms and antonyms, as shown in Figure 5-2. Some word processors even let you replace the word in the document with a word from the list. No more paging through the thesaurus, and mulling over what category to look under.

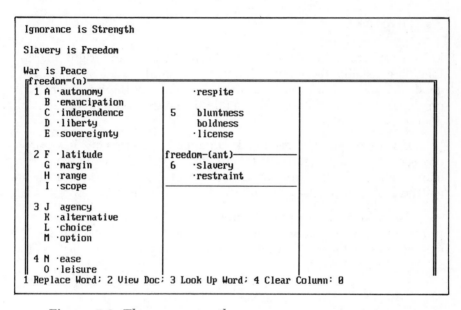

```
Ignorance is Strength

Slavery is Freedom

War is Peace
freedom=(n)
  1 A ·autonomy              ·respite
    B ·emancipation
    C ·independence     5    bluntness
    D ·liberty               boldness
    E ·sovereignty          ·license

  2 F ·latitude         freedom-(ant)
    G ·margin           6    ·slavery
    H ·range                 ·restraint
    I ·scope

  3 J  agency
    K ·alternative
    L ·choice
    M ·option

  4 N ·ease
    O ·leisure
1 Replace Word; 2 View Doc; 3 Look Up Word; 4 Clear Column: 0
```

Figure 5-2. The on-screen thesaurus.

Page Formatting

Once you have the content of your document under control and you've fixed all your typos and misspellings, you can start working on the appearance of your document—how you want it to look on paper. Here is a list of some of the formatting options that most word processors offer:

▶ Set left/right margins

▶ Number pages

▶ Right-justify the text

▶ Center a word, line, or block of text

▶ Set page length

▶ Set top/bottom margins

▶ Create headers and footers

▶ Prevent widows and orphans

Setting Margins

Most programs offer default settings for the left and right margins; these are usually the standard, most commonly used settings. It's a good idea to use these settings until you see how the document looks on paper. You can then go back and change the settings to adjust the document.

66

If your program offers block commands, it probably has one for changing the margin settings for a single block. Since it's so easy to change margins, play around with different margin settings until you get the look you want—you can always change them back.

To make your document appear more attractive in print, word processors leave blank space at the top and bottom of each page. You can make these top and bottom margins as large or as small as you like.

Numbering Pages

In the past, numbering document pages was a tedious process. First, you had to remember to number each page. Then, you had to make sure you typed the correct number in some consistent location.

With the word processor, the program automatically numbers the pages for you, keeping the pages in sequence, positioning the numbers in the same place on each page, and making sure the numbers are in the same format throughout. You can even specify the way the number is displayed—for example, -1-, 1, Page 1, #1, etc.

One of the advantages of automatic page numbering is that it gives the computer a point of reference for printing. If you find a mistake on one of the pages after printing it, enter the correction and have the program print out only the page with the correction.

Right-Justifying

If you like the way a newspaper column looks, with the words aligning perfectly at the right margin, you can choose to *right-justify* your document. The program automatically inserts the necessary space between characters or words, spreading the text to the right margin.

Centering Text

Centering text on most typewriters is a chore. With the word processor, just type the word or sentence and tell the program to center it between the margins. This is great for creating your own letterhead or setting titles.

Setting Page Length

67

Most word processors assume you'll be printing on 8 1/2-by-11 inch paper. If you're using the longer legal size paper, just specify the length of the page, and the program makes the necessary adjustments. If you're using the automatic page numbering feature, the program even renumbers the pages.

Creating Headers and Footers

You can type the title of your document, your name, the date, or anything you like and have the program print it on the top or bottom of every page of the document. If the information is printed on the top of the page, it's called a *header*. At the bottom of the page it's called a *footer*. Figure 5-3 shows some examples.

Widow and Orphan Protection

Until you print your document, you can't be sure of where the program will end one page and start another. Because of this, you can end up with the first line of a paragraph at the bottom of a page (a *widow*) or the last line of a paragraph at the top of a page (an *orphan*). An example of each is shown in Figure 5-4.

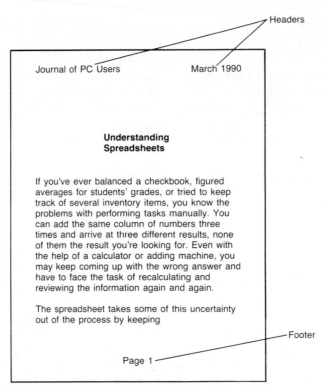

Figure 5-3. Headers and footers.

To prevent this problem, some programs offer widow and orphan protection. This feature automatically prints widows on the next page and moves orphans to the previous page.

Working with Columns

Most word processors display text across the width of the page, but you may want to format the text in columns. Some word processing programs can create up to six columns per page and can adjust the columns automatically to accommodate changes. Figure 5-5, shows a document in the column format.

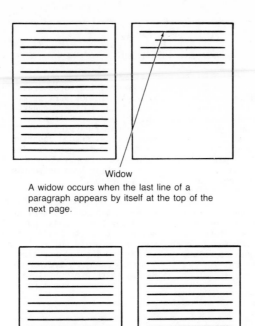

Widow

A widow occurs when the last line of a paragraph appears by itself at the top of the next page.

Orphan

An orphan occurs when the first line of a paragraph appears by itself on the previous page.

Figure 5-4. Widows and orphans.

69

Character Formatting

In addition to formatting the entire page (arranging and rearranging the big picture), word processors let you work with the smaller elements, the characters that you type. Depending on the range and capabilities of your printer, you can use some software that produces amazing effects.

```
                    Gulliver's Travels
                         Part I
                 A Voyage to Lilliput
                        Chap. I

     My father had a small      was recommended to several
estate in Nottinghamshire; I    patients. I took part of a
was the third of five sons. He  small house in the Old Jury;
sent me to Emanuel College in   and being advised to alter may
Cambridge at fourteen years     condition, I married Mrs.
old, where I resided three      Mary Burton, second daughter
years, and applied myself       to Mr. Edmund Burton, hosier
close to my studies: but the    in Newgate street, with whom I
charge of maintaining me        received four hundred pounds
(although I had a very scanty    for a portion.
allowance) being too great for
a narrow fortune, I was bound       But, my good master Bates
apprentice to Mr. James Bates,  dying in two years after, and
an eminent surgeon in London,   I having few friends, my
with whom I continued four      business began to fail; for my
years; and my father now and    conscience would not suffer me
then sending me small sums of   to imitate the bad practice of
money, I laid them out in       too many among my brethren.
learning navigation, and other  Having therefore consulted
D:\CHAPTER.ONE                                 Doc 1 Pg 1 Ln 1" Pos 4"
```

Figure 5-5. Many word processors give you the ability to divide a page into columns.

To highlight key words and phrases, many word processors let you select from various *typestyles* and *fonts*. A typestyle simply enhances the normal type that your printer puts out. For example, boldface, italics, and underlining are all typestyles; the character's design stays the same, but one aspect of it is changed. A font, on the other hand, is a set of characters that deviates from the normal type, and is labeled by its *typeface* (design) and size (measured in *points*)—for example, Helvetica 12-point. (Just for reference, there are 72 points in an inch.) Figure 5-6 shows various fonts.

By using different typestyles and fonts, you emphasize titles and paragraph headings, set off sections of text, and produce attractive letterheads and documents.

> ► **Tip:** If you're shopping for software that includes special typestyles and fonts, make sure your *printer* can keep up with the *program*. Although most printers can handle one or two typestyles (boldface and underline), many printers simply cannot handle varieties of fonts.

Italicized text   <u>Underlined text</u>

Shadow text   Condensed text

Geneva   New York

Venice   **Chicago**

Helvetica   Monaco

Outline text

Extended text

Times

Courier

Bookman

Figure 5-6. Word processors display text in a variety of styles and typefaces.

71

Additional Formatting Tools

In addition to all the formatting elements mentioned above, word processors may offer several tools to help you visualize your formatting before you print the document and to save you the work of redesigning your format every time you want to use it.

Saving Your Format in a Stylesheet

Most people use the same three or four formats for whatever written documents they produce. If you have to recreate the format for every document, you not only waste time but also risk the possibility of leaving something out. Fortunately, you can save the format specifications to a *stylesheet* or to a separate file to use later.

Stylesheets can define line and paragraph spacing, indentation, fonts, type size, and typestyle. While you create a document, you can concentrate on the writing without having to worry about appearance. When you've finished, the stylesheet formats your document.

What You See Is What You Get (WYSIWYG)

What you see on screen may look nice and tidy, but when you print it, the margins may be misaligned, there may be too much space between paragraphs, and the typestyles may not have printed as you expected.

To help you anticipate these problems, several programs offer a feature called WYSIWYG (pronounced "wizzywig")—What You See Is What You Get. This feature does display the document exactly as it will print.

Figure 5-7 is an example of what you see when you don't have WYSIWYG. This is WordPerfect's Reveal Codes screen showing the typestyles specified for each word, the line spacing, the paragraph indents and so on.

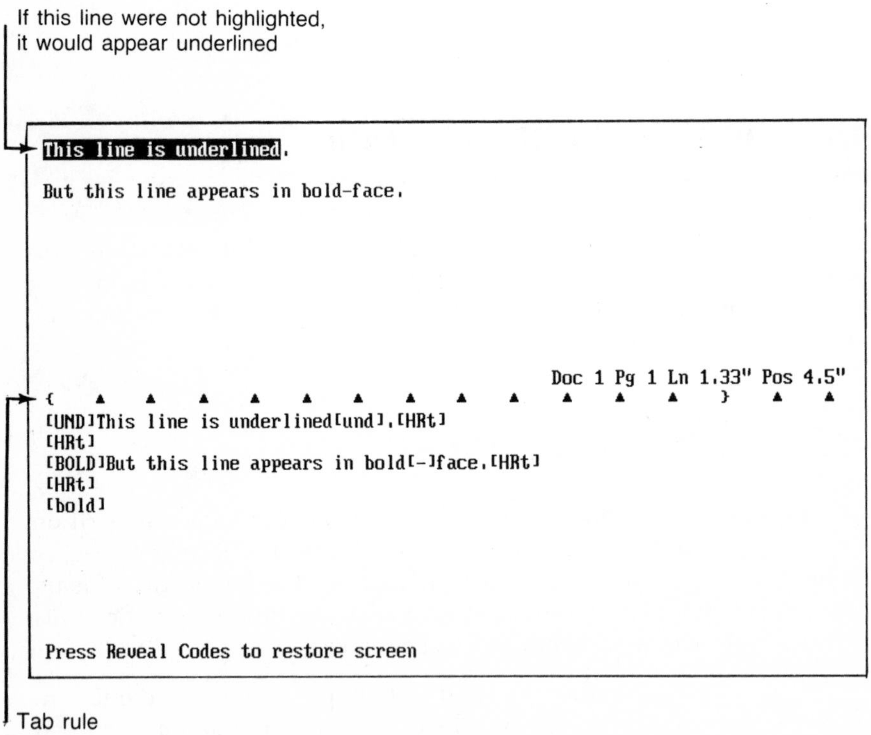

72

If this line were not highlighted,
it would appear underlined

```
This line is underlined.

But this line appears in bold-face.




                                              Doc 1 Pg 1 Ln 1.33" Pos 4.5"
{   ▲   ▲   ▲   ▲   ▲   ▲   ▲   ▲     ▲   ▲   ▲   }   ▲   ▲
[UND]This line is underlined[und].[HRt]
[HRt]
[BOLD]But this line appears in bold[-]face.[HRt]
[HRt]
[bold]




Press Reveal Codes to restore screen
```

Tab rule

Figure 5-7. WordPerfect's Reveal Codes screen.

Page Preview

When you write with a typewriter or pad of paper, you can see exactly what your page looks like as you write. Not so with word processors. Usually, the word processor displays only a section of the page—you need to scroll up and down or use your imagination to see any more than that.

Some programs offer a preview feature that displays the document on screen before printing it. This feature usually provides two views of the page: *full-page* (bird's eye) and *close-up*. With full-page you can't make out the words, but you can see if a page comes up short, if it has widows or orphans, or if its layout is just plain ugly. With the close-up view, the page is usually not quite as sharp as what will be printed, but it gives you some idea of how a font looks in context and whether a large font will interfere with surrounding text. Figure 5-8 shows a sample preview screen.

73

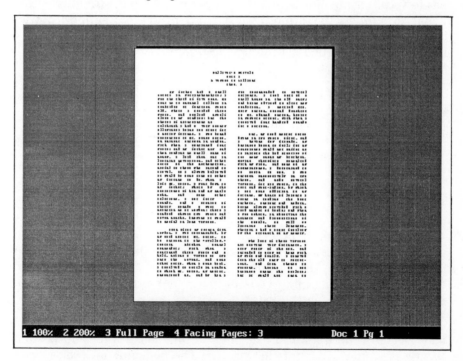

Figure 5-8. A page preview screen.

Printing Your Document

You've done all the hard work—the writing, editing, formatting, and reformatting. All you need to do now is send your final creation off to the printer to have all those electronic characters transformed into a real live version of your document.

Printer Support

Printing your document essentially consists of sending the file to the printer. The printer uses the information from the file to determine what characters to print, and then prints those characters to paper.

In order for this process to work, the word processing program has to speak in a language that the printer understands. In other words, it has to *support* the printer. Most word processors support a wide range of printers; all you need to do is specify the printer you're working with. This is called *setting up the printer*.

> ▶ **Tip:** When you're shopping for software, check to make sure that the *program* supports your *printer*. If it doesn't, you may not be able to use the program with your printer or you may not be able to use all the fonts and typestyles that your printer supports.

When you begin to enter commands to print a document, the program asks you to select from a list of printers that the program supports. If your printer is not on the list, you can often choose a printer from the list that acts like your printer. Your printer is then said to *emulate* the printer on the list.

If your printer does not emulate a printer on the list, the program may give you the option of selecting an unlisted printer and customizing the printer setup for that printer. The customizing process consists of entering ASCII commands that tell the program how to work with the printer. You can find these ASCII commands in the manual that comes with your printer.

Merging Information from Two or More Files

Sending a file to the printer gives rise to one of the most powerful features associated with printing—the *merge* feature. With this feature, you can create a document and type *embedded commands* telling the program to insert specific pieces of information. You can then merge this document with another file that contains the information you want to insert. The program reads information from both files and prints a single document, inserting the information you specified in the blanks.

You can use this feature to insert graphs or tables from one file into a report from another file or to print several chapters of a book (each one a separate file) as a single document.

One of the most impressive uses of this feature reveals itself when you merge a form letter with a database containing hundreds of names, addresses, and other information. As illustrated in Figure 5-9, it's a simple four-step process:

75

1. Create a form letter and indicate where you want specific information inserted.
2. Tell the program where to find the information to enter (a drive or a directory).
3. Tell the program which records in the file you want to print letters for. For example, you can tell the program to print letters to all people whose last name begins with "K" or to all people living in Indianapolis.
4. Tell the printer to start printing.

Special Word Processing Features

Most of the features explained above are fairly common. There are other features that make your work even easier. You might want to keep them in mind when you're shopping.

Automatic Backups and Auto-Save

We mentioned earlier that it's a good idea to back up your files in case anything happens to the original. Many programs offer a feature that

John Smith
123 Main Street
Anycity, CA 92011

Mary Douglas
5555 Emerald Street
Sea Breeze, CA 92540

Joseph Flagenbaum
3 C Avenue, #304
Costa Verde, CA 93092

Database

Dear <First> <Last>,
   Congratulations! The <Last> family has already
won $500 cash, a microwave oven, or a cordless
telephone. All you need to do is call 1-800-555-1234
to claim your prize.
   Imagine the surprise the residents of <City> will
feel when they hear that you have a unique opportunity to take advantage of this vacation resort. Over
a thousand other people in the state of <State>
have already taken advantage of this offer. Why not
call today?

Form letter

Dear John Smith,
   Congratulations! The Smith family has already won
$500 cash, a microwave oven, or a cordless tele-
phone. All you need to do is call 1-800-555-1234 to
claim your prize.
   Imagine the surprise the residents of Anycity will
feel when they hear that you have a unique opportunity to take advantage of this vacation resort. Over
a thousand other people in the state of CA have
already taken advantage of this offer. Why not call
today?

Figure 5-9. A database and form letter merging.

does this for you. If you make a mistake and delete a file, return to the backup copy and start over.

> ⃠ **Warning:** Don't rely completely on automatic backups. They're stored on the same disk as the original. If you lose or damage that disk, both files are gone. It's still good practice to copy the file on a separate disk and store it somewhere safe.

Another form of protection that some word processors offer is an auto-save feature that automatically saves your work at specified intervals. Every five, ten, or fifteen minutes, or after you haven't typed anything for awhile, the program automatically saves the changes you just entered to disk. If you find that you're too busy typing to worry about saving your work, consider getting a program that offers this feature.

Windows

Windows let you divide a screen into two or more parts. Each window can contain different files or different parts of the same file, giving you the added advantage of seeing files together in one of two different formations—overlapping and tiled (see Figure 5-10). If you combine the block command feature and mouse support with windows, you can create a powerful editing tool. You can use the mouse to highlight a block of text in one document, point to the place in the other document where you want the block inserted, and Bingo! the job is done.

Graphics

If you have the merge feature and a graphics program, you can insert the graphics you create in that program into your documents. Refer back to Figure 5-5. It showed graphics elements mixed with text to form a simple newsletter.

In addition to that, however, some word processing programs offer graphics features that let you create simple line drawings within the text. Some programs may provide a list of shapes that you can choose from and modify for your own use. For example, the menu may provide a box that you can stretch in either direction to suit your use.

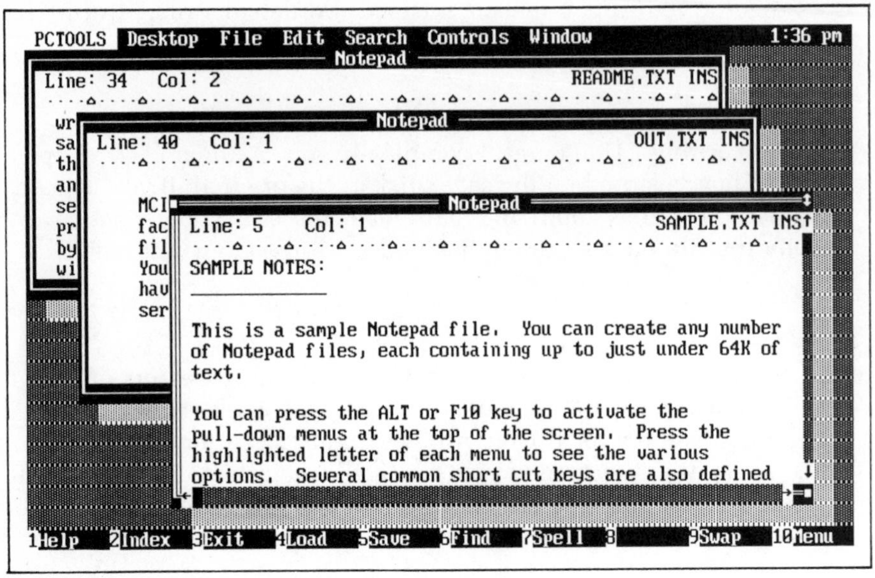

(A) Overlapping

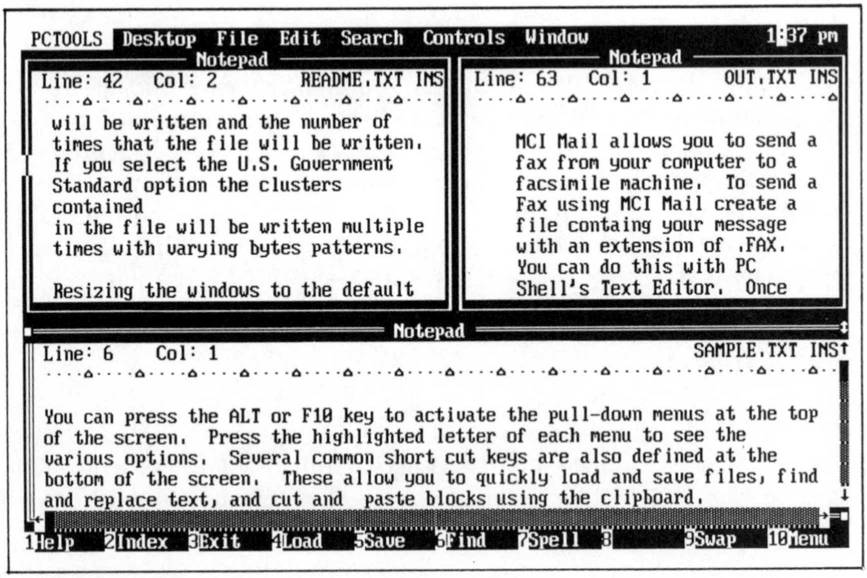

(B) Tiled

Figure 5-10. The two ways of displaying multiple files in windows.

Although these basic word processing graphics are not designed for high-quality illustrations, you can use them to improve the appearance of your reports, to create simple flow charts, or to draw boxes around important blocks of information.

Import/Export Files

Word processors store files in different formats; for example, if you write a letter using WordPerfect, you cannot edit that same file using Microsoft Word. Because so many people use different word processing programs, sharing files can be difficult. To overcome this difficulty, many word processors can save or retrieve files in different formats. With programs that offer this feature, you simply tell the program what format the file is in, and when the program opens that file, it automatically converts the file to the format you're using.

79

> ▶ **Tip:** Because WordPerfect and Microsoft Word are available for both IBM and Macintosh computers, you can create a file on an IBM, transfer the file to a Macintosh, then edit that same file using the Macintosh version of WordPerfect or Microsoft Word.

Automatic Indexing

If you're writing a report that requires an index, you could search through your entire document page by page. Whenever you found a word that you wanted to include in the index, you could keep a separate list and note all the pages where that word appears.

Tedious? Of course, and that's why the computer can do it so well. All you do is tell the program the key words, terms, and concepts that you want to include in the index. The program searches every page and creates a list of indexed words complete with the page numbers where they appear.

Computer Shorthand: Macros

As you get faster and faster on the word processor, you will begin to notice that you perform several of the same tasks fairly often, and these tasks may require you to enter several commands. Whenever you notice such a pattern developing, or you're getting frustrated entering the same commands, it's a good sign that you need a *macro*. A macro is simply a record of several commands assigned to a two-key keystroke. Think of it as a programmable telephone that dials a complete phone number when you press a single button. For example, you may need to perform the following four steps to print a document:

1. Open a menu.
2. Choose the Print command from the menu.
3. Specify the name of the printer.
4. Press Enter.

80

To save yourself time, you could record these commands and assign them to a keystroke, say Ctrl-P for "print document." Whenever you wanted to print the document, you would simply press Ctrl-P instead of entering the four commands. You can use macros to store complete addresses, commonly used phrases, and other information that you type regularly.

While macros retype previously typed keys, abbreviations work like shorthand. Instead of typing a complete word, such as "Massachusetts," you could type the abbreviation "MA" or any abbreviation you choose. After you are through writing, the word processor converts all your abbreviations to the complete spelling according to a list that you provide. If you don't have this feature, you can use the search and replace feature to take advantage of abbreviations.

Counting Your Words

If you need to generate a word count for whatever reason, many word processing programs offer a word count feature that can help out. Besides counting words, some word processors may also count the number of sentences and paragraphs in a document and analyze the document to determine an estimated reading level. For example, if you're writing training manuals and your audience has a sixth-grade reading level, this feature tells you if the structure and word choice of your document is appropriate.

Basic Math

To add a column of numbers contained in a report, a word processor may offer mathematical capabilities that can add, multiply, subtract, or divide numbers. When you change the numbers in your document, the word processor automatically recalculates the new result.

By providing simple math capabilities, word processors let you create reports with columns of numbers that you do not have to calculate by hand. For more complicated reports, a spreadsheet is easier to use (see Chapter 6).

Many word processing programs offer a Calculator *utility* as well. This utility works just like a regular calculator except that it's displayed on-screen.

Outlining

81

With the outlining feature, you type certain characters (such as *, 1., +) that tell the program to indent the line. The program automatically lays out the outline for you.

With some word processors you can create an outline heading and type a paragraph beneath the heading. When you want to move the paragraph, just move the heading within the outline.

Tables

Tables are a great way to present lists of related information side by side. Although you can create tables using any word processor, editing tables in some programs is a pain. If a program doesn't offer special formatting elements to keep the entries separate, deleting one entry in a table can mess up the entire table.

Some word processors, however, offer a table feature that treats each table entry separately. That way if you add or delete an entry, other entries are not affected.

What You've Learned

Word processing programs enable you to create professional, attractive documents or manuscripts with maximum flexibility and efficiency. There are many commercial programs to choose from, so do your research before you shop. In general, these are the basics:

▶ Word processors let you create documents in four simple steps: type the document, edit it, format it, and print the final product.

▶ The cursor lets you move around your document and enter corrections.

▶ Block commands let you move, copy, or delete a block of text or change the line spacing or font of an entire block.

▶ Most word processors let you undo a deletion.

▶ You can have the word processor check your spelling throughout an entire document and search and replace every occurrence of a word, term, etc.

▶ Page formatting lets you position your document on the page, number the pages, print on different page sizes, add headers or footers, and avoid widows and orphans.

▶ You can format characters to set off words, phrases, headings, or even entire sections of text.

▶ The merge feature lets you combine information at the printing stage to generate a single, unified document.

▶ Page preview lets you "print" the document on screen before you print it on paper.

▶ When you're shopping for software, make sure the program you choose supports the printer you're using and the fonts that the printer supports.

▶ Many word processing programs offer additional features, such as auto-save, windows, outlining, and automatic indexing that can make life a lot easier.

82

Chapter 6

The Electronic Spreadsheet

In This Chapter

▶ *Understanding the electronic spreadsheet*
▶ *Working with numbers*
▶ *Using a spreadsheet to balance your books*
▶ *Generating graphs*
▶ *Creating comprehensive reports*
▶ *Using the spreadsheet to predict the outcome of a change*

If you've ever balanced a checkbook, figured averages for your students' grades, or kept track of product inventory, you know the problems with performing the tasks manually.

With a very simple format, the spreadsheet enables you to do the job quicker, more efficiently, and with a reduced risk of human error. First, you set up a template that can perform a series of calculations automatically as you enter the numbers.

Once you set up this template, you no longer have to worry about the calculations. If you make a mistake entering a number, you can go back, change only that number, and tell the spreadsheet to recalculate the result—whether you change one number or thousands of numbers.

Because the spreadsheet can recalculate so quickly, you can use it to play "what if." "What if I mark up the price of my widget by an additional 5%, how would that affect my profit?" "What if I gave each of my employees a $100 bonus?" You can plug in any number you like and see the effects.

In addition, most spreadsheet programs let you create graphs to analyze the relationships between different variables. For example, you can graph your profits over a period of time to determine patterns or trends that may help you plan for the future.

Spreadsheet programs may also offer *linking* so that two or more spreadsheet files share information. If you change a number in one file, the spreadsheet automatically recalculates any changes in other files.

84 Understanding the Spreadsheet

As with any application program, you must open a file before you can start working. When you open a file in a spreadsheet program, the program displays a screen that provides you with a basic outline. The spreadsheet is a lot wider and longer than what you see on screen at one time. (See Figure 6-1.)

Let's examine this screen. At the top is a ruler with letters that represent *columns*. Along the left side of the screen are numbers representing *rows*. A spreadsheet can consist of as many as a hundred columns and rows. The point where a column and row intersect forms a rectangle, called a *cell*.

Each cell has an *address* made up of the combination of the column letter and the row number. For example, the cell that's formed by the intersection of column D and row 12 has the address D12. You can *label* the columns and rows with meaningful headings, so you don't have to guess what the letters mean.

The screen displays some indicators that tell you what's going on. There's a status bar that may tell you something you should do. Scroll bars and arrows help you to move around in the spreadsheet. A current cell indicator tells you the address of the cell the cursor is in, known as the *active cell*.

Cell addresses are important, because you use them to construct the formulas you want to calculate. For example, you may have a row

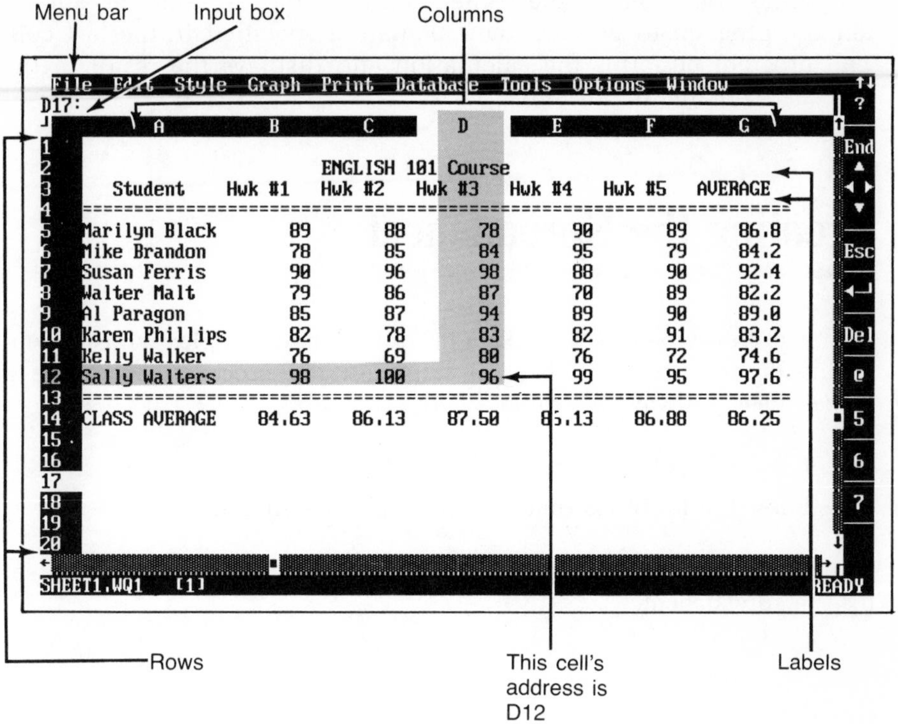

Figure 6-1. A typical spreadsheet.

of cells that contain the grades for one student. Refer to Susan Ferris in Figure 6-1. She has five grades entered in cells B7 through F7. Although you cannot see it now, the cell at the end of the row (in G7) contains the formula:

B7 + C7 + D7 + E7 + F7 / 5

This formula tells the spreadsheet to enter a value in this cell that is an average of the values in cells B7 through F7, so the spreadsheet enters **92.4**.

> ▶ **Note:** This example is a little longer than it needs to be; you can usually use a shorthand version like SUM (B7..F7)/5 to perform the same calculation.

After you enter all the student's grades for the semester, simply tell the program to perform the calculation specified in the last cell. The program performs the calculation and displays the result in the cell that contains the formula.

Creating the Spreadsheet

Although the spreadsheet can be a fairly large and complex monster consisting of hundreds of cells and formulas, the process for creating a spreadsheet is always the same:

1. Label the columns and rows.
2. Enter the formulas that the spreadsheet will use.

86

You don't have to worry about the numbers until after you've set up the spreadsheet.

Moving the Cursor

In the upper left-hand corner of the spreadsheet is a shaded rectangle; this is your cursor. This cursor fills an entire cell, and the contents of that cell are usually displayed in an *input box* on the screen. To change the contents of a cell, you usually need to change the contents in the input box and then press Enter to insert the new information. The spreadsheet moves by jumping from cell to cell.

Table 6-1 shows some common commands for moving the cursor in a spreadsheet. Although these commands are specifically for Lotus 1-2-3, many spreadsheet programs share the same commands. When you first start using a spreadsheet program, practice a little with the cursor movement keys before doing anything else. When you're comfortable with the commands, you can move on to the serious work of creating your spreadsheet.

Table 6-1. Cursor Movement Commands for Lotus 1-2-3

Press	To move the cursor
Right/Left Arrow	One column right/left
Up/Down Arrow	One row up/down
Ctrl-Right Arrow or Tab	One screen right
Ctrl-Left Arrow or Shift-Tab	One screen left
PgUp/PgDn	One screen up/down
Home	To the upper left corner of the spreadsheet
End-Up Arrow	To the topmost cell containing data
End-Down Arrow	To the bottommost cell containing data
End-Right Arrow	To the rightmost cell containing data
End-Left Arrow	To the leftmost cell containing data
F5	To a specific cell by address

Getting Started

When you get pretty good at moving the cursor around, you're ready to begin laying out the basic structure of your spreadsheet. If you have a form that you want the spreadsheet to look like, lay the form down by your keyboard and use it as a model. For example, if you're going to use the spreadsheet to balance your checkbook, use your most recent bank statement or your checkbook to set up the columns and rows.

Entering Labels and Formulas

When you have some idea of the basic structure of your spreadsheet and the tasks you want it to perform, you're ready to begin. The first thing you need to do is enter labels and formulas as shown in Figure

6-2. Labels are common-sense headings for your columns and rows. Formulas are the calculations you want your spreadsheet to perform. Notice that each formula consists of the address of at least one cell and a mathematical symbol that performs some operation on that cell.

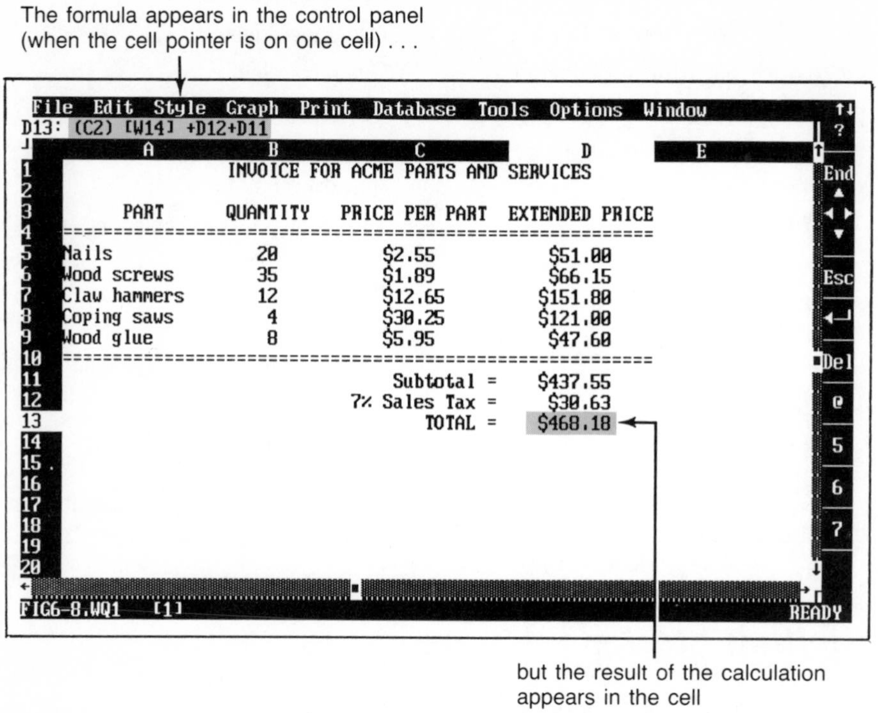

The formula appears in the control panel
(when the cell pointer is on one cell) . . .

but the result of the calculation
appears in the cell

Figure 6-2.   Cell D13 contains a formula to determine the invoice's total.

The labels and formulas may be wider than the initial columns displayed on screen. To accommodate these labels, or any long line, the program provides a feature that either widens the column or simply displays as much as it can in the column. You can adjust column width to fit any labels, or leave columns narrow in which case only the first word or so of the label shows up.

Let's take a closer look at the spreadsheet in Figure 6-2. Notice that it uses several formulas that build on one another:

▶ The formula in cells D5 through D9 multiplies the *number of parts* by the *price per part* to determine the *extended price.*

▶ The formula in D11 totals the extended prices in cells D5 through D9 to determine a subtotal.

▶ The formula in D12 multiplies the subtotal by the tax rate to determine sales tax due.

▶ The total formula in cell D13 adds the tax (from cell D12) to the subtotal (from cell D11) to determine the total amount due.

Because formulas can use the address from any cell containing a value, the formulas can use addresses of cells that contain previous formulas. This is what gives the spreadsheet so much power and flexibility.

The lesson in this is that you don't need one long formula that takes care of everything. The spreadsheet works the same way, breaking the calculations into stages to make them easy to manage.

Using the Spreadsheet's Functions

Creating simple formulas such as adding two numbers is a piece of cake, but creating a formula for the one-period depreciation of an asset using the straight-line method is chore. To help you in such cases, many programs offer predefined formulas called functions. Some of the more common functions are listed in Table 6-1. If you're working with statistical process control, the statistical function is a must. Special accounting programs, such as DacEasy and Peachtree Complete, provide an exhaustive repertoire of financial functions.

Table 6-2. Spreadsheet functions

Functions	Calculations
Mathematical	Absolute values, logarithms, square roots, and trigonometric equations
Statistical	Averages, maximum and minimum values, standard deviations and sample variance
Financial	Compounding periods, the internal rate of return, straight-line depreciation allowance, and number of payment periods in an investment

Sometimes a simple formula is not enough. For instance, if you sell a product in several states and you cannot charge sales tax on out-of-state sales, you need a *conditional formula* that tells the program, "If the items are being shipped within the state, calculate the sales tax; if not, charge no sales tax."

Figure 6-3 shows an invoice for a manufacturing company in Indiana. The conditional formula here says, "If the shipment is being shipped to a company within Indiana, charge 5% sales tax; if not, calculate a 0% sales tax." The formula appears as:

IF(B7="IN",D18*0.05,0)

That is, "If the entry in cell B7 is IN (Indiana); then multiply the subtotal in cell D18 by .05 (5%); if not, then enter 0 (zero)."

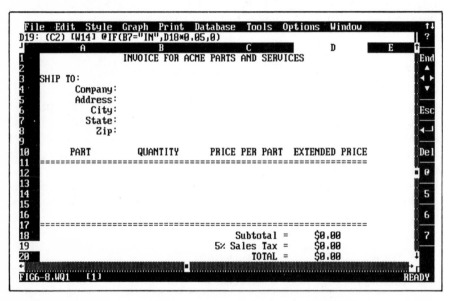

Figure 6-3.   A sample invoice with a conditional formula.

A *validation* restricts an entry in a cell to a particular value or range of values, preventing you from making big mistakes that could hurt you financially or legally. For example, you could use a validation for petty cash that prevents you from entering a withdrawal over $100.

Formatting the Cells

Once you have the basic layout of your spreadsheet under control, you can format the cells, telling the spreadsheet how to display the data. Do you want commas inserted in numbers over 999? Do you want to display dollar signs next to monetary values? Do you prefer dates displayed as 09-01-91 or as 09/01/91?

Formatting also lets you set your column and row headings in a different typestyle, such as bold, to set the headings off from the data. You can even right-justify the labels to align them with the data. Simply mark the cells you want to format and enter the command from the keyboard or menu to activate the format.

> ▶ **Tip**: When you've finished designing your spreadsheet, it's a good idea to save the basic *template* (labeled rows and columns with formulas entered) in a separate file. That way, whenever you need to enter numbers into the spreadsheet, you'll have a blank form to start with.

Performing a Test Run

When your spreadsheet is complete, and you're fairly sure it'll work, it's time to perform a test run, which verifies that it meets three requirements:

▶ you have all the rows and columns you need

▶ the columns are wide enough

▶ the spreadsheet works

To perform a test run, enter simple numbers in each cell that requires them—numbers that let you calculate the results quickly in your head so you can check the performance of your spreadsheet. Be sure to use numbers that are about as wide as the ones you'll be entering.

Even when you're careful, something can go wrong, and it can be difficult to see just what the problem is. If you perform your dry run and you're getting an error message or some crazy-looking values, check for the following problems:

Order of Operations. Each spreadsheet performs its calculations in a particular order, usually from left to right, performing multiplication and division first and then addition and subtraction. You can change the order of operations by using parentheses. Make sure your formula is in the proper order and the parentheses are positioned correctly.

Forward References. If you use formulas that rely on previous formulas for their calculations, check to make sure that no formula uses the formula in a later cell to perform its calculations. A cell can only use a formula from a *previous* cell.

Circular References. A circular reference occurs when a formula uses its own results as part of a calculation. The spreadsheet goes around in circles trying to find the answer, but never succeeds.

If something doesn't work, go back and correct it immediately, and then perform another dry run until the spreadsheet works.

> ▶ **Tip:** Be sure to check the spreadsheet thoroughly before you start using it on real numbers. If you discover a *bug* (problem) in the spreadsheet after you've already used it to perform several calculations, you could have a lot of work ahead of you.

Entering the Raw Data

When you're absolutely certain that your spreadsheet works, get the raw data that you want to calculate, and start plugging in the values. When you're done, go back and double-check the values you entered. Then enter the command to calculate, and the spreadsheet displays all the results, as shown in Figure 6-4.

```
File  Edit  Style  Graph  Print  Database  Tools  Options  Window        ↑↓
D19: (C2) [W14] @IF(B7="IN",D18*0.05,0)                                    ?
      A           B              C            D           E        ↲
1                    INVOICE FOR ACME PARTS AND SERVICES                  End
2                                                                          ▲
3  SHIP TO:                                                              ◄ ►
4        Company: Northwind Inc.                                          ▼
5        Address: 123 Main Street
6           City: Carmel                                                 Esc
7          State: IN
8            Zip: 46032                                                   ↲
9
10      PART          QUANTITY    PRICE PER PART  EXTENDED PRICE         Del
11 ================================================================
12 Nails              20          $2.55           $51.00                  @
13 Wood screws        35          $1.89           $66.15
14 Claw hammers       12          $12.65          $151.80                 5
15 Coping saws        4           $30.25          $121.00
16 Wood glue          8           $5.95           $47.60                  6
17 ================================================================
18                             Subtotal =         $437.55                 7
19                         5% Sales Tax =         $21.88
20                               TOTAL =          $459.43
FIG6-8.WQ1   [1]                                            READY
```

Figure 6-4.   *Results of spreadsheet calculations.*

Graphing the Data

Most spreadsheet programs can use the information from your spreadsheet to create graphs automatically. These are a big help in analyzing the results of your spreadsheet calculations. All you have to do is enter a few commands covering:

▶ Information you want included in the graph

▶ Kind of graph you want to use: bar graph, line graph, pie chart

▶ Legends to explain some elements in the graph

▶ Symbols to use for points: periods, x's, dashes

After you specify all the formatting features for the graph, the program displays the graph on screen so you can view it, and often lets you save the graph in a separate file or print it out immediately. Figure 6-5 shows various types of graphs.

94

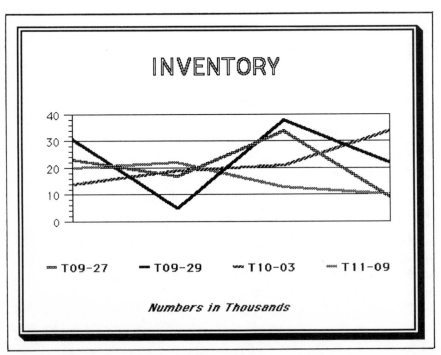

(A) Bar graph

(B) Line graph

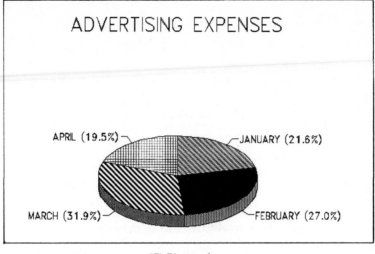

(C) Pie graph

95

*Figure 6-5. Three types of graphs you can create with a
spreadsheet program.*

Printing the Finished Spreadsheet

When you finally have all your numbers entered and the spreadsheet
has performed the calculations, it's time to print the spreadsheet to
send or to keep in your records. Most spreadsheets require that you
specify at least a few parameters for printing. The program may display
a printer setup screen asking you to

▶ Specify which spreadsheet you want to print and where you
want the printing to start. For example, the program may print
everything below where you position the cursor.

▶ Choose the destination for the spreadsheet. You can print the
spreadsheet to a disk, to screen, or to your printer.

▶ Define a header. The spreadsheet may let you type a header for
your spreadsheet, including a title, page number, and date. The
program usually numbers the pages of a single spreadsheet
automatically.

▶ Define the page layout. You have to enter margin settings and
tell the program the size of the paper you want to print on. (See
Figure 6-6.) Since spreadsheets can be very wide, most programs let you print a spreadsheet on legal size paper turned

sideways. This is referred to as *landscape orientation*, as opposed to the normal, *portrait orientation*.

▶ Indicate how many copies you want to print.

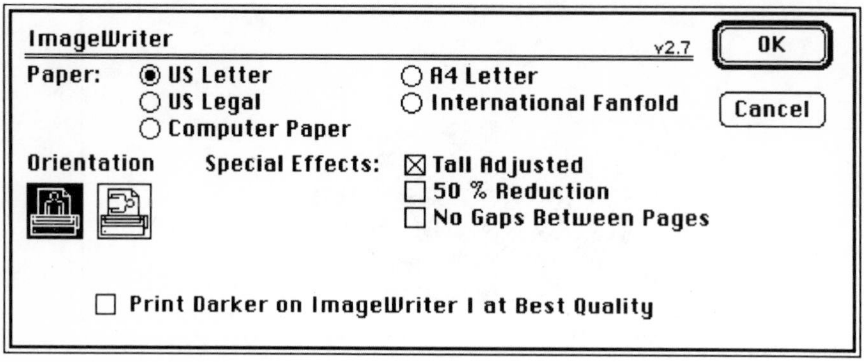

Figure 6-6. A Macintosh printer setup dialog box that lets you define how you want to print your file.

96

After you enter these settings, simply enter the print command for the program you're using.

Special Spreadsheet Features

Most of the features mentioned above are fairly common among spreadsheet programs. There are additional special features that can make working with spreadsheets easier, and are worth the extra price.

Seeing the Big Picture Through Windows

The size of your computer screen limits how much of the spreadsheet you can see at any one time. This can cause problems when you want to see how a change you enter at the beginning of your spreadsheet affects the bottom line. Or, you may need to see how a change on an invoice affects your inventory spreadsheet.

In such cases, it helps to have a split screen, and that's exactly what windows provide. With windows, you can do the following:

▶ Display two sections of the same spreadsheet on screen at one time.

▶ Display two or more spreadsheets on screen at once.

▶ Make one window larger or smaller than the other.

▶ Switch from one window to the other to enter information. This is great if you need to enter information from one spreadsheet to another.

▶ Zoom in on the active spreadsheet so that it takes up the entire screen.

▶ Stack windows in layers so you can see the title of each spreadsheet at one time.

▶ "Tile" the windows so a miniature version of each window is displayed.

Taking Shortcuts with Macros   97

You may have many spreadsheets that use the same labels and formulas. Some programs offer *macros* to spare you the tedium of retyping the same data for each spreadsheet.

You can record common strings of characters and commands and play them back with a single two-key keystroke. If you're working with a menu-driven program that requires you to open several menus to enter a command, create a macro that opens all the menus for you and chooses the command.

Remember all those parameters you had to define to generate a graph? You could set up a macro to perform those steps automatically. Assign a two-key combination to the macro, such as Ctrl-G, and you're all set. Next time you want to generate a graph, just hold down Ctrl (Control) and type **G**. Better yet, have the macro create *and* print the graph, saving you all the steps for specifying printer settings.

You can also use the macro to *capture* a string of characters. Just enter the command for your program to start recording your keystrokes, and type the entry as you would normally type it—for example, **Acme Services, Western Sales Region**. Enter the command to save the macro, and that's it. The next time you need to enter that company's name in a spreadsheet, move the cursor to the cell you want to enter the information in, and press the two-key combination you assigned to the macro.

When you've finished creating the macro, you can save it to disk to use in other spreadsheets.

File and Command Compatibility

File compatibility means that one spreadsheet program can use the data created and stored in another spreadsheet program. Because Lotus 1-2-3 has been the standard spreadsheet for so long, many competing spreadsheets offer compatible software. In addition, programs may offer *command compatibility*. For example, one program may offer the same commands as Lotus 1-2-3 and add several fancy commands in an attempt to go beyond 1-2-3.

> ▶ **Tip:** Be careful when shopping. If you can buy a fancy new spreadsheet, make sure it's compatible with your old spreadsheet so that it can manipulate the data without your having to re-enter the numbers. Get a spreadsheet that's compatible with the version of spreadsheet you're presently using or a later version. If you have Lotus 1-2-3 version 3.0 and you buy a spreadsheet that offers compatibility with version 2.2, you may not be able to use all of the Lotus files you need.

Auditing

Earlier, we mentioned common problems with formulas, such as forward and circular references. These bugs can be very difficult to find, especially if you've created a complex maze of formulas. To help you, some programs offer an *auditing* feature that displays the problem on screen.

Setting Goals

You've already seen how you can use a spreadsheet to play "what if" with numbers. By changing entries and recalculating the sheet, you can see the results of a possible change. Some programs offer a feature that does the opposite—the goal-setting feature. You change the bottom line, and the spreadsheet changes the entries to show you what you must do to meet your goals.

Linking

Spreadsheets can be extremely large, making them difficult to manage. *Linking* lets you break down these large spreadsheets into smaller units to give you more control. By seeing a portion of the spreadsheet, you can often see the relationships between numbers more clearly rather than being overwhelmed by the big picture. Any changes you enter in one of these portions ripples through the other portions as well, keeping the whole intact.

Multidimensional Spreadsheets

99

Although linking spreadsheets can help you manage your spreadsheets, they are still limited to two dimensions. For example, you can use the spreadsheets to analyze the number of purchases per customer, but you cannot analyze those same purchases over several months.

To give your information a third dimension, you need to use a multidimensional spreadsheet. This spreadsheet essentially stacks several spreadsheets on top of one another in the same file. You then have more flexibility in how you choose to analyze the information. For example, you can still see a comparison of purchases per customer, but now you can analyze the history of purchases for a single customer over several months. If the customer has been making fewer and fewer purchases, you know there's a problem.

Turbocharging Your System

You can run basic spreadsheets with the simplest hardware, but if you plan on using spreadsheets for most of your work, you may need a few of these extras before you can really take off:

▶ Additional memory
▶ Math coprocessor
▶ Mouse support

> **Tip:** Spreadsheets are vats full of information. If you don't have sufficient RAM, you may not be able to use some of the larger IBM spreadsheets. If you don't want to shell out the money for additional RAM, keep your spreadsheets small and link them together as explained earlier. Without the extra RAM, the system will be mighty slow.

If you use your spreadsheets to play "what if" or to set goals with large, complex spreadsheets, you might consider getting a computer with a *math coprocessor*. The coprocessor calculates the same equations within seconds that it takes minutes for the standard processor installed in your computer to do.

A mouse lets you point to the cells you want to change, format, or modify. Instead of using the cumbersome arrow keys to move around the spreadsheet, just point to the cell you want to change and press the mouse button. If you want to mark several cells to change their format, stretch the highlight over an entire block of cells and enter the formatting command of your choice.

Combine the mouse with a system that supports windows and you can move information from one window to another with the click of the mouse.

What You've Learned

This chapter has explained spreadsheet basics but given you a mere glimpse of the spreadsheet's power. When you get the opportunity to work with some of the predesigned spreadsheets that are on the market, you'll be amazed at how much work they can save you and how fast they perform their chores. Until you get that chance, make sure you understand the basics:

▶ A spreadsheet is a grid consisting of rows and columns that intersect to form cells.

▶ Each cell has a unique address that's made up of a letter (representing the column) and a number (representing the row).

▶ Formulas perform calculations on the values in the cells. Each formula consists of one or more cell addresses and a math operator.

▶ Before you begin using your spreadsheet, you should perform a test run and work out any bugs.

▶ You can use a spreadsheet to play "what if"—to see the results of a change before you invest in effecting the change.

▶ Most spreadsheet programs let you graph the information contained in a spreadsheet so you can analyze the data.

▶ If your spreadsheet program offers windows, you can use the windows to display two or more sections of the same spreadsheet or two or more spreadsheets at the same time.

▶ Macros let you enter several commands with a single two-key keystroke.

▶ A math coprocessor and additional RAM can make your spreadsheet program perform its calculations much faster.

101

▶ You can break large spreadsheets into smaller units and link the units to make the spreadsheet run faster.

Chapter 7

The Electronic Database

In This Chapter

▶ *Understanding the database*
▶ *Using the database to sort records*
▶ *Finding records at the touch of a key*
▶ *Printing lists and mailing labels*
▶ *Creating reports*

A database is a collection of records that contain individual entries. A doctor, for example, may create a database by having all patients fill out a standard form during their first visit. The doctor could then use this database to find all the patients with high blood pressure and send them updated information on their condition.

Popular database programs include dBASE III Plus, Paradox, Oracle (*relational databases*) and Q&A, FileMaker Pro, and Reflex (*flat-file databases*). We explain the differences between relational and flat-file databases later in this chapter, but for now you just need to know that relational databases are expensive and capable of handling large amounts of information. Flat-file databases are less expensive and more suitable for handling smaller amounts of information.

Creating a Database

You begin compiling your database by creating a *form*—a template that lets you fill in the blanks with information. The blanks in this case are referred to as *fields*. By entering information into the fields, you create *records*. A record is a collection of information about a single topic; it may contain the specifications for a gear or the name and address of a client. Figure 7-1 illustrates the structure of a database.

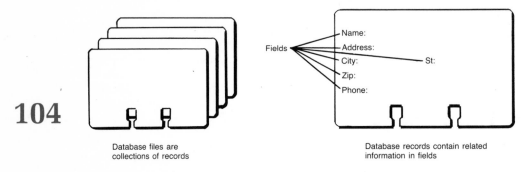

Database files are
collections of records

Database records contain related
information in fields

Figure 7-1.   The basic structure of a database.

The database uses the field names to identify information. If you want to sort the records, for example, simply tell the program to sort them according to the entries in one of the fields. If you want to lift some information from a record and insert it into a letter, type the field names in the letter. The database retrieves the specified information and inserts it into your letter. (We'll look at this in more detail later.)

Designing the Form

Designing the form requires a great deal of foresight. You need to anticipate what information you will need, approximately how long the maximum entry in each field will be, what kind of information will be entered in each field (characters or numbers), and what is the clearest, most succinct wording for your field names.

To make these decisions, refer to the non-computer system you're presently using—your Rolodex, phone book, calendar, list of employees, accounts receivable, inventory list, etc. Think up field names for each piece of information you'll need. Weed out any unnecessary information—you don't want to turn your database into a junkyard.

When you're designing the form, keep a few guidelines in mind:

▶ If you're using the database to store information such as invoices or purchase orders, include a field that gives each record a unique number. This lets you sort and find records easily.

▶ Be logical. Your form should present information in a natural flow, from left to right and top to bottom, in the order that you use it.

▶ Leave blank space for entering data to the right of the field name, not below it. Leave sufficient space for your entries.

▶ Keep field names just long enough to explain the entry that follows. Long field names take space away from your entries and may cause problems when you need to use them in form letters.

▶ If an entry can be typed a number of ways, include an example of how you want it entered—for example, Date(mm/dd/yy). That way, if you can shove the data entry work onto some other poor soul, they'll type the information the way you want it to appear.

105

The Opening Screen

Whatever database program you have, you must enter a command for creating a form. When you open the file, you see a screen similar to the one shown in Figure 7-2. The name of the file you just opened is at the top right. The screen also indicates which page of the form you're working on. (Forms can be 1 to 60 or more pages, depending on the program.)

The top line down is a menu bar that lists pull-down menus you can access. You type your field names and entries below this line. If the line is a list of pull-down menus, it usually includes a help menu.

The bottom of the screen usually displays some indicators that tell you what's going on. For example, there may be a prompt telling you what you need to do (*Type field name*), and some databases show a ruler indicating where the cursor is positioned. This ruler is important in that it can help you align the field names on your form. The screen may also contain a menu bar at the bottom, if there wasn't one at the top.

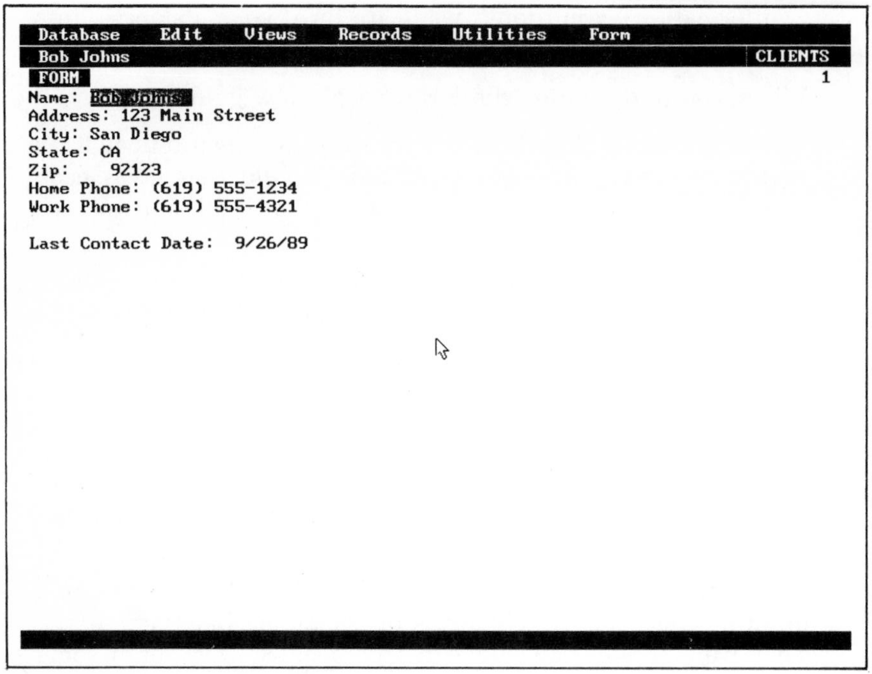

Figure 7-2. The opening screen for a database program.

Usually, when you're designing your form, you move the cursor just as you would in a word processing program, using the arrow keys and other commands. You'll probably make more use of the Tab key than usual, because you'll be concerned with aligning your field names.

After your form is created, the cursor takes on some different movements, letting you skip over the field names and go right to the fields to type your entries. To move from one field to the next, press the Tab key. To move to a previous field, press Shift-Tab.

Typing the Field Names

Typing the field names is no complex task. Just type as you normally would, leaving plenty of space for the entries you'll be typing later. Remember, keep them short, but not so short that you'll forget what they mean. When you're typing field names, you may want to press your Caps Lock key to type the names in all uppercase letters. That way, you can easily see where the field name ends and the field entry begins. Figure 7-3 shows a completed form. Note all the additional space left for the address and notice that the field names are aligned.

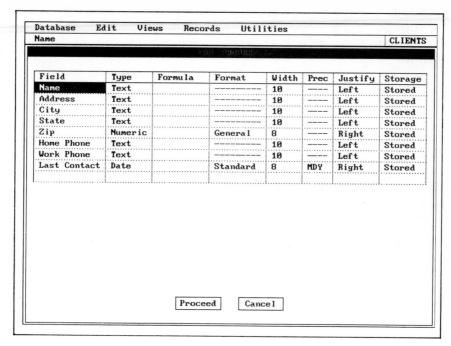

Field	Type	Formula	Format	Width	Prec	Justify	Storage
Name	Text		————	10	——	Left	Stored
Address	Text		————	10	——	Left	Stored
City	Text		————	10	——	Left	Stored
State	Text		————	10	——	Left	Stored
Zip	Numeric		General	8	——	Right	Stored
Home Phone	Text		————	10	——	Left	Stored
Work Phone	Text		————	10	——	Left	Stored
Last Contact	Date		Standard	8	MDY	Right	Stored

Figure 7-3. The create form screen with formatting codes entered.

Formatting the Fields

When all your fields are in place, you can start to plan how you want the information you enter to appear on the form. For example, you can have the program convert whatever date you enter into a predetermined format. Type **Sept. 4, 1991** in the DATE field, and the date appears as *09/04/91*. Type **3125679876** in the PH# field, and the phone number appears *(312) 567-9876*.

Database programs that offer formatting features require you to enter a specific code for the format you want. For example, to have the date appear as mentioned above, type **mm/dd/yy** in the DATE field on the screen used for creating the form.

Using Field Attributes

In addition to specifying formatting codes, you usually have the option of entering *field attributes* that give the form special information about the entry in a particular field. A few common field attributes are listed below:

> *Index.* You can add field attributes, such as 1, 2, 3, to have the database generate an index for specific fields. These indexes help you work with the information in a particular field by focusing on the information only in that field.
>
> *Unique Data Entry.* You can tell your database that every entry in a particular field must be unique. For example, if you're entering purchase orders, you want a different purchase order for each form. If you try to type an entry that's the same as another one, the program displays a message telling you so.
>
> *Default Entries.* If you're doing business exclusively in one city or state, you can specify a default entry that will be entered in that field for every record you create. This saves you the trouble of entering the same information over and over.

> ▶ **Tip:** Make sure the form is just as you want it before you start creating records. Some programs offer a way for you to edit field names later and reorient your database, but even in these cases you need to be careful.

When you've put all this care and preparation into creating a form, you hardly want to have to re-create it later, so be sure to save it. Your database program saves the form in a separate file so that none of the field entries you type later will affect the form itself.

Typing Field Entries

Typing field entries is the least challenging, most time-consuming part of creating a database. Here's where you enter all the information that you want to include in the database—names, addresses, company contacts, part numbers, prices, and inventory lists.

To type field entries, move the cursor from field to field and type the required information. You're simply filling out the form. You don't have to enter information into every field, but if you don't enter information into a field and you use the database to search for a record according to what's entered in that field, you're out of luck!

Be sure to check the entries on screen against your source. It's pretty easy to edit field entries later, but if you enter Jehnson when you meant to enter Johnson and you try to find Johnson's record later, your database won't know what you're looking for.

Save the record. This usually consists of typing a single command as indicated on your screen. The program saves the information you entered, and displays a blank form, ready for you to create your next record.

Continue filling out forms until all the information you need in your database is entered. Remember, back up your database by copying it to another disk.

109

Using the Database

Now that you have this oversized filing cabinet sitting in your computer, how do you go about getting at those records? You have at least three options:

▶ Browse through the records one at a time
▶ List the information in every record according to field name
▶ Search for a specific record or range of records

Browsing through your records is the most basic method of viewing your records, but browsing is fairly slow and useful only for finding a record when you don't know what record you want to find.

If you list the information from one or more fields in each record you can view a list of sales representatives and their sales figures. Just enter the list command and tell the database which field entries you want listed (see Figure 7-4).

This list also serves as a directory, and you can enter a display command to display the entire record of one of the records on the list.

```
 Database    Edit    Views    Records    Utilities    List
 1/01/89                                                      SALES
 LIST                                                            1
          Date   Rep        Product    Quantity   Sales $  Avg Pric  Unit Cos
 ▶    Jan-89   Alan       Paddles          81    $6,550     $81       $77
          Jan-89   Alan       Silent           16   $16,835    $1,052    $570
          Jan-89   Alan       Sport            10    $4,976     $498      $390
          Jan-89   Alan       Swiftwater        9    $6,672     $741      $437
          Jan-89   Bob        Paddles          51    $5,235     $103      $77
          Jan-89   Bob        Silent            6    $6,450    $1,075    $570
          Jan-89   Bob        Sport             7    $3,794     $542      $390
          Jan-89   Bob        Swiftwater        9    $7,433     $826      $437
          Jan-89   Cathy      Paddles          45    $4,613     $103      $77
          Jan-89   Cathy      Silent            7    $6,709     $958      $570
          Jan-89   Cathy      Sport             5    $2,667     $533      $390
          Jan-89   Cathy      Swiftwater        7    $5,728     $818      $437
          Jan-89   Dave       Paddles          68    $6,325     $93       $77
          Jan-89   Dave       Silent           12   $11,760     $980      $570
          Jan-89   Dave       Sport             9    $5,831     $648      $390
          Jan-89   Dave       Swiftwater       16   $11,836     $740      $437
          Feb-89   Alan       Paddles          85    $6,635     $78       $77
          Feb-89   Alan       Silent           17   $16,317     $960      $570
          Feb-89   Alan       Sport            11    $5,477     $498      $390
          Feb-89   Alan       Swiftwater       14    $9,244     $660      $437
          Feb-89   Bob        Paddles          41    $4,583     $112      $77
          Feb-89   Bob        Silent            3    $3,267    $1,089    $570
```

Figure 7-4.   A list of records according to field entries.

Searching for a single record is the fastest and easiest way to find a specific record or group of records. If you enter a command telling the database to search, it responds by asking what you want to search for.

All you need to do is type whatever you want to look for in the field where that information is located. The entry you type is referred to as *search criteria*. For example, if you want to find out about how many paddles your sales representative Alan sold in a particular time period, you could enter information as shown in Figure 7-5.

The program finds the specified record and displays it on screen, as shown in Figure 7-6.

If the search criteria you entered matches the field entry in several records, the program displays the first record it finds (in this case Alan's March sales appear first). You must then browse through subsequent records.

If you need to view a range of records, say purchase order numbers 10013 to 10078, or companies with outstanding invoices of $300

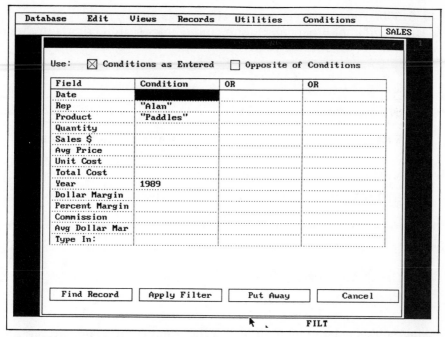

Figure 7-5.   *A search screen.*

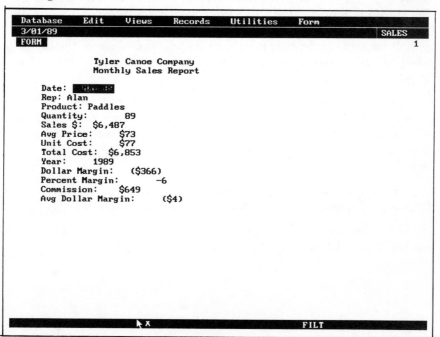

Figure 7-6.   *At the end of the search, the database displays the record.*

111

to $1500, you can enter the specific range in the field you want to search. Different programs require you to enter search criteria in different formats (see Table 7-1).

Table 7-1. *Searches within a Specific Range*

Search Criteria	Finds
K>W	Words beginning with K through W, but not A through J
<=50	Numbers 50 or less
=3/16/1991>3/31/1991	Any record from March 16th to March 31st of 1991

112   *When You Don't Know What You're Looking For*

After you've entered a hundred or a thousand records, no one can seriously expect you to remember the exact spelling of every entry in every field. You'll forget a few, and you need some way of finding these records. That's why most database programs let you use *wild cards* to search for records. In poker, wild cards take the place of the cards you need to make a hand. In this case, wild cards stand in for particular characters you can't remember.

There are two types of wild cards. One kind represents any *single* character in the same position. The other kind represents any *group* of characters in the same position. Common wild card characters are asterisks, question marks, and ellipses, depending on the program you're using.

In Table 7-2, a question mark is used as a single character wild card and ellipsis points represent a group of characters.

All you need to do is type the wild card entry in the proper field and send the database on a search.

Table 7-2. Wild card Searches

Wild Card Entry	Finds	Does Not Find
?age	page, sage	mortgage
?ook	book, took	shook
?ook?	books, looks	bookend
...Smith	Smith, John Smith	Smithson
Smith...	Smithson	John Smith
...Smith...	John Smith, Smithson	Smythe

Editing and Deleting Records

Once you're comfortable with the search criteria and search commands for the particular program you're using, everything else is a piece of cake!

113

To edit a record, display the record on screen and use the same keys you used to edit information on a word processing screen. Some programs offer special commands that let you delete an entire field entry or all the entries in a single record. Some even let you edit the information in a single field for several records at once.

To delete a record, just call it up on screen, and enter a delete command. Use the delete command in tandem with the search criteria to delete an entire group of records with a single command. Many programs offer a recall feature that lets you get back deleted records, but you should be careful anyway.

Like the word processor, many databases offer a search and replace feature that lets you find and replace every occurrence of a name, date, or figure in a particular field with the new entry you specify. If the city where most of your clients reside decides to change its area code from (312) to (708), simply type the old entry and tell the database which records you want the change to affect. Unleash the search and replace feature, and seconds later, you have an entire revised database.

Sorting Your Records

As you enter records into your database, the database stores the records in the order that you enter them. If you entered a stack of records in no particular order, your database is a mess. If you call up a list of records, they appear in no logical order. Luckily, the database sorts your records in whatever order you specify and presents you with a neat, orderly stack.

Is this significant? It sure is. Just look at what you can do with the sort feature:

> *Sales Analysis.* Sort the records for your sales force to determine who's selling the most goods and making you the most profit.
>
> *Ranking.* Rank students by grades to determine the most effective mix for group activities.
>
> *Follow-Ups.* Sort invoices by date due, so you can find out who has owed you money for the longest time. Sort by total amount due to find out who owes you the most money.
>
> *Bulk Rates.* Print out form letters grouped by ZIP code to take advantage of bulk rates.
>
> *Rosters.* Print out a list of employees or clients by phone number to create telemarketing lists.

114

Like the search feature, the sort feature requires you to enter criteria in whatever field you want to sort. For example, if you want to sort your records by last name, you might type **1** in the LAST NAME field or enter a command, such as

SORT ON LAST_NAME TO ALPHA

telling the program to sort the records according to the entry in the LAST NAME field and store the index in a file called ALPHA.DBF.

Since some records may contain the same entry in the field you choose to sort, many programs let you enter sort criteria in more than one field. The criteria entered in the first field is called the *primary sort criteria*, and the criteria entered in the second field is referred to as the *secondary sort criteria*. If there's a tie, the database looks to the entry in the secondary field to determine how to sort the records. Figure 7-7 shows a sort screen with sort criteria entered.

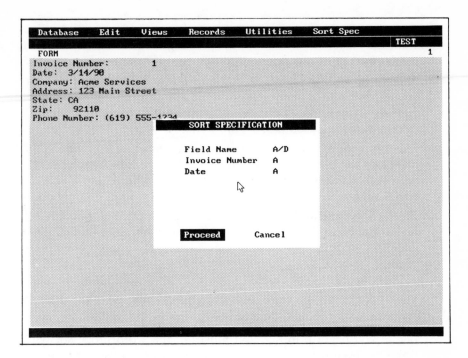

Figure 7-7.   A sort screen that sorts the records first by invoice number, then by date.

115

Notice the *A* in the Invoice Number field. This indicates ascending order. When you're entering sort criteria, you usually have to specify whether you want the records sorted in ascending order (A, B, C...1, 2, 3) or descending order (Z, Y, X...10, 9, 8), and whether you want them sorted alphabetically or by number. Otherwise, the program sorts the records according to its default setting (usually alphabetical ascending order).

Generating Form Letters, Reports, and Mailing Labels

You've seen how much power the field names give you in searching and sorting your records, but that's not the half of it. You can also use the field names to yank information out of your records and consolidate it in a single location:

Form Letters. Create a generic letter and type field names where you want to insert information. Then merge your letter with your database to print out customized personal letters (see Figure 7-8).

Reports. Set up a sheet with several column headings that correspond to the field names in your database. Merge the sheet with your database to create a comprehensive report containing all of the information you need (see Figure 7-9).

Mailing Labels. Create a single mailing label consisting of field names in the place of actual names and addresses. Merge the label with your database to print an entire roll of mailing labels in a matter of minutes.

Analysis. Search and sort to find which product your company sells makes the most profit in specific sales regions. As a bonus, search and sort to find which salesperson sells the most of a specific product.

116

The asterisks tell the word processing program to go to the database, find the necessary information, and insert it into this location.

Before you begin printing, you must tell the word processor where to find the information and which records you want to use. The program automatically finds those records, inserts the necessary information from each record into a separate letter, and prints the letters in the order you specified.

> ▶ **Tip**: The only hard part of printing mailing labels is convincing your printer that it's printing on tiny sheets of paper (the labels). You need to fiddle with the margin and page length settings before you get it just right (you may want to jot down the settings so you don't have to fiddle next time)—and don't forget to enter your sort and search criteria.

Choosing the Right Database for You

Database programs vary in how they structure the database and what special features they offer. That's not to say that one is better than the other. You just need to find the one that's right for your needs and budget.

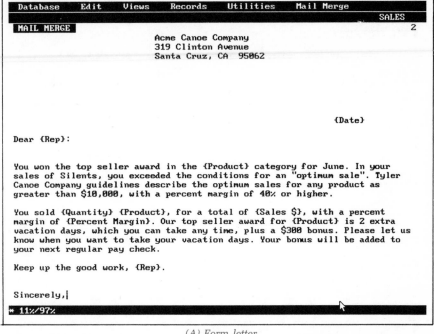

(A) Form letter

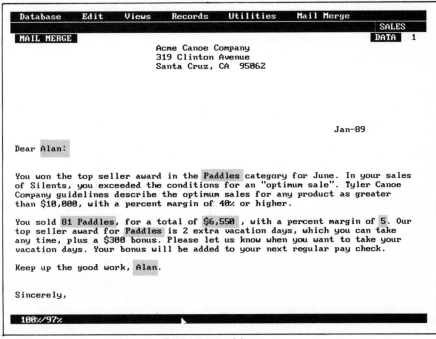

(B) Customized letter

Figure 7-8. Printing customized personal letters.

```
Database    Edit    Views    Records    Utilities    Attributes    Report
                                                                   SALES
REPORT DESIGN
▼ Introduction ················································································
                    ACME CANOE COMPANY SALES              █
                       January - June 1989

▼ Header ·····················································································
▼ Preview 1-Date ·············································································
Date              Rep              Product           Total Sales

▼ Preview 2-Rep ··············································································
▼ Detail ·····················································································
   Date           Rep              Product            Sales $
▲ Detail ·····················································································
▲ Summary 2-Rep ··············································································
                                                      ──────────
                       Total Sales for     Date:    =@SUM(Sale

▲ Summary 1-Date ·············································································
▲ Footer ·····················································································
▲ Conclusion ·················································································




Row:2 From Col:52 Through Col:52
```

(A) Template

```
Database    Edit    Views    Records    Utilities    Attributes    Report
                                                                   SALES

                    ACME CANOE COMPANY SALES
                       January - June 1989

Date              Rep              Product           Total Sales

  Jan-89          Alan             Paddles             $6,550
                  Alan             Silent             $16,835
                  Alan             Sport               $4,976
                  Alan             Swiftwater          $6,672
                  Bob              Paddles             $5,235
                  Bob              Silent              $6,450
                  Bob              Sport               $3,794
                  Bob              Swiftwater          $7,433
                  Cathy            Paddles             $4,613
                  Cathy            Silent              $6,709
                  Cathy            Sport               $2,667
                  Cathy            Swiftwater          $5,728
                  Dave             Paddles             $6,325
                  Dave             Silent             $11,760
                  Dave             Sport               $5,831
                  Dave             Swiftwater         $11,836
                                                      ──────────
                       Total Sales for Jan-89:        $113,414

Date              Rep              Product           Total Sales

  Feb-89          Alan             Paddles             $6,635
                  Alan             Silent             $16,317
                  Alan             Sport               $5,477

Continue previewing page 1?    Continue    Quit
```

(B) Report

Figure 7-9. Generating customized reports.

You can choose from among three types of databases: flat-file and relational databases, mentioned at the beginning of this chapter, are more powerful and offer greater flexibility. A third type, *free-form*, is easier to use and less expensive.

The Free-Form Database

Unlike a filing cabinet containing folders neatly arranged in drawers, a free-form database mimics the random pile of notes you might find cluttered on a desk (see Figure 7-10). Some popular free-form databases include AskSam and MemoryMate for IBM and compatible computers.

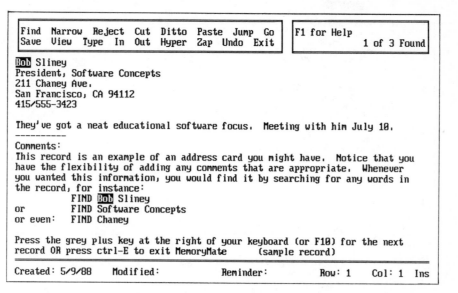

Figure 7-10. The structure of the free-form database.

The free-form database consists of records with field entries, but without fields, so you're not limited to the type of information you can enter. You can use the database to store reports, spreadsheets, names and address, and any other information.

The hard part is finding that information once you've stored it. Since you don't use field names to structure the database, the database has no way of finding information that matches a certain criteria or inserting it into form letters and reports.

The Flat-File Database

A flat-file database works like a Rolodex (see Figure 7-11). Each record in the file contains the same type of information entered in standard fields, such as names, addresses, and telephone numbers.

120

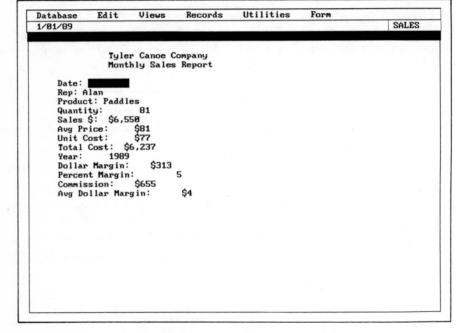

Figure 7-11. The flat-file database.

Flat-file databases are excellent for storing information to print mailing labels, but fall short in generating comprehensive reports. Flat-file means that the database can only use one file at a time. If you want to join a separate SALES file and a PROFIT file to form a comprehensive report analyzing sales versus returns, you can't. Some popular flat-file databases include Q&A, FileMaker Pro, PC-File, Reflex, and RapidFile.

The Relational Database

A relational database is the most powerful type of database because it can use two or more database files and combine them into a new, separate file.

Most accounting programs use a relational database. Each database file is a separate module, such as Invoicing, Purchase Orders, Payroll, and Inventory, that interfaces with a General Ledger module that oversees the entire operation, as shown in Figure 7-12.

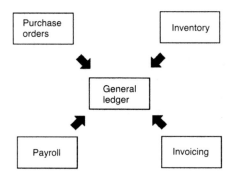

Figure 7-12. **The relational database in accounting software.**

121

Whenever you *post* a transaction, the transaction is recorded to the General Ledger that then enters the transaction into all the other files (modules) that the transaction affects. For example, if you sell six widgets to one of your customers and send the customer the required invoice (the bill), you enter the transaction in the Invoice module only. The program automatically subtracts the six widgets from the inventory module. The program may even tell you when you need to order more widgets.

The relational database not only pulls all your database files together, it helps you analyze information from several files by producing comprehensive reports and graphs that compare and evaluate the information. Popular relational databases include dBASE III Plus, Fox-Pro, Oracle, Paradox, R:Base, 4th Dimension, and Double Helix.

> **Tip:** Besides general purpose database programs, you can also buy specialized databases for storing such diverse topics as genealogical information, appointments, and office management. The advantages of specialized programs is that you only need to plug in the information. The disadvantage is that if you don't like the way the program works, you can't change it.

Special Features

In addition to the different structures of the various databases, some offer special features that make them easier to use, including

122

Automatic field length adjustments

English language assistant

Command files

Shortcuts

Graphs

Command and file compatibility

One of the most difficult parts of setting up a form is guessing how long the longest field entry will be. No matter how much space you leave, there's always someone with a last name of 25 characters. To help in these cases, some programs offer fields that you can stretch when you need more room. You may need to enter a command to view the entire contents of the field, but at least it lets you fit in all the information you need.

> **Tip:** Many databases offer a special English language assistant. Rather than type cryptic commands to the database like **2FIND Name = "Smith" or Salary > $25,000**, type the English sentence, **Find me all the Smiths who make more than $25,000 a year**. This saves you the trouble of looking up the command in your User's manual or accessing a help screen.

Command files are a lot like macros. Instead of having to type a long series of commands each time you want to perform a task, such as printing mailing labels, you can store the steps in a command file. When you want to perform the task, simply play back the file.

Some programs offer a *compiler* that lets you turn your command files into separate programs to make them run faster. You can use these new separate programs independent of the database program, share your custom programs with others, or use them in other databases without carrying the extra baggage of the database program.

Many databases offer unique commands that help you perform some of the more common database tasks in less time with fewer commands. For example, the program may offer a command to graph the data entered in a particular field or a setup that makes it much easier to print mailing labels.

Graphs convert database information into easy to understand pictures that help you analyze data more clearly.

123

Because the most common database program for IBM and compatible computers is dBASE III Plus, many people have stored large amounts of information in dBase files. Rather than retype all this data into a new database program, people would rather continue using their existing files, and for good reason! Because of this, many new database programs are specially designed to use dBASE III Plus files. Such programs are said to be dBASE III Plus compatible.

What You've Learned

A database is a vast electronic resource where you can store and retrieve names, addresses, inventory figures, stock prices, real estate records, schedules, and anything else that can be listed and stored. It's a Rolodex, telephone book, accounting ledger, and filing cabinet all rolled into one. When you create the databases that are customized for your needs, keep the following points in mind:

▶ A database consists of several records containing field entries.

▶ You can format the fields on a form to display information uniformly.

▶ Field attributes let you enter special instructions or default field entries into your form.

▶ You should edit your form thoroughly before using it to generate records. Editing the form later may make some information inaccessible.

▶ When you save a record, you're storing information in your database.

▶ You can search your database by browsing page by page, by generating an index of your records, or by entering search criteria for a specific record or range of records.

▶ To sort your records, you must enter sort criteria, telling your database which fields to use for sorting and whether to sort in ascending or descending order.

▶ Field names give you the power to pull information from your database and insert it into a single location. This lets you generate comprehensive reports, personalized letters, and mailing labels.

124

▶ Free-form databases are best for storing random thoughts and data. Because they lack a structure, sorting and searching data can be difficult.

▶ Flat-file databases store structured information and can be easy to use, but cannot combine data from two or more files. This means you may have to type identical data in separate database files.

▶ Relational databases are the most powerful, letting you share data between several files.

Chapter 8

Computer Graphics

In This Chapter

- ▶ *Understanding graphics programs*
- ▶ *Assembling basic shapes to produce complex illustrations*
- ▶ *Modifying shapes and objects with the press of a button*
- ▶ *Stacking objects on-screen*
- ▶ *Saving sketches in files, and reusing them in new illustrations*
- ▶ *Modifying and assembling old drawings to create new ones*
- ▶ *Computer transparencies*

You can plan the most beautiful drawing in the world, but if the execution fails—if the ink bleeds, if the perspective is off a hair, if you shade too darkly in one area or draw a line slightly too thick—the drawing just doesn't make it.

That's why graphics programs are so useful. You plan the drawing, think about the composition and the perspective, and then draw a rough draft on-screen. Save the draft to disk, and retrieve it whenever you want to work with it.

Instead of *redoing* the draft, you *modify* it. You alter the perspective, change line thicknesses, add or delete details, all on-screen. You can even combine several basic shapes to create a single, complex illustration.

You don't commit the drawing to paper until it's absolutely perfect, and when you do, you use a plotter or printer that's less likely to introduce errors than a shaky, tired hand (see Figure 8-1).

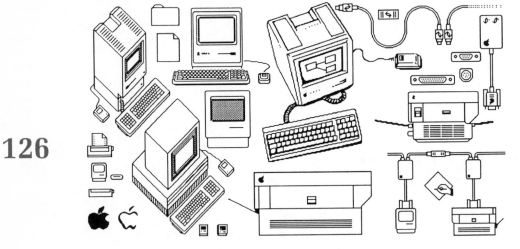

Figure 8-1. A computer-generated illustration.

Understanding Graphics Programs

Your computer screen is essentially a canvas made up of 150,000 to 200,000 luminous dots called *pixels*. Whenever you type a character or draw a line, you activate a series of these pixels so that they form a recognizable shape on-screen.

Drawing with Graphics

A *draw program* lets you create line drawings using objects like circles, ovals, squares, and lines. By combining these objects together, you can make flow charts, technical illustrations, graphs, and organizational charts.

Since a drawing consists of objects, you can easily modify your drawings by changing the position, size, or line thickness of each object in the drawing.

The most popular draw program for the IBM is CorelDraw. To use this program you need at least an IBM AT or compatible, a mouse, and a copy of Microsoft Windows. The most popular draw program for the Macintosh is MacDraw.

Painting with Graphics

A *paint program* lets you control the position of each pixel on your computer screen, giving you more control over your painting, but also making it more difficult to edit entire sections of your painting with one command.

By painting each pixel on the screen, you can create finer details than you can with a draw program (see Figure 8-2). Of course such detailed control also means that editing a painting requires detailed (and sometimes tedious) work as well.

127

Figure 8-2. Paint programs give a more three-dimensional look.

One of the most popular IBM paint programs is PC Paint. The most popular Macintosh paint programs are MacPaint and SuperPaint. SuperPaint offers both paint and draw features, so you can combine the best features of each in a single illustration.

Because graphics programs give you greater control over your screen and make more use of the pixels than do other programs, you should have a mouse or similar instrument to take advantage of this increased flexibility. The mouse moves the cursor across the screen just as a pencil moves across paper.

> **Tip:** Think twice about cutting corners with your printer. If you're going to create fancy sketches for commercial purposes, make sure you have a high-quality printer that does justice to your work.

Creating an Illustration

Graphics programs are usually based on a two-point system. You define two points on the screen and then specify what sort of line you want to connect the two points.

The stable point appears as a single dot. The point that you adjust is displayed as a cross hair. By moving the cross hair away from the stable point, you *stretch* a line across the screen. If you tell the program to connect the two dots with a circle, you can stretch the circle to whatever dimensions you need.

Once you have some basic shapes constructed, you can assemble, manipulate, and enhance those basic shapes to create complex illustrations.

Basic Lines and Shapes

All drawings are made up of three types of lines: straight, curved, and irregular. The line tool takes care of the perfectly straight lines, the curve tool lets you draw geometric curves, and the pencil tool lets you draw the irregular shapes.

The Line Tool

The line tool is basically a ruler; you can't draw curves with it. Creating a line is a simple process of stretching the line across your screen.

To draw a line, move the cursor to the place where you want the line to start; this is the beginning point of the line. Choose the line tool from the Tools menu or enter the line draw command; the mouse pointer changes to the cross hair symbol. Click the mouse button to define the starting point for the line, then drag the cross hair to the place where you want the line to end. Click the mouse button once again to define the end point of the line, and that's that; the line tool automatically connects the dots.

Most programs also let you choose different patterns or styles of lines to help you create fancy borders for reports or presentations.

The Curve Tool

The curve tool also lets you mark the beginning and end points of a line and then join these points with a line segment. In this case the line segment is a curve. You specify the points, then select the degree of curve you want from the menu. The curve tool automatically links the points with the specified curve and you can even fill in the curve with a pattern.

129

The Pencil Tool (Freehanding It!)

The pencil tool gives you more control over your line. You're still drawing a line, but this time you don't have to follow the edge of a ruler or the curve of a circle.

To use the pencil tool, choose it from the Tools menu, or enter the required command. Click the mouse button to define the starting point of the line; you'll see the now-familiar cross hair. Draw curves, straight lines, loop-the-loops, you name it. Just remember to click the mouse button when you've finished playing.

Templates

In addition to tools that let you create your own basic shapes, programs also offer several predesigned shapes that you can plop down on your screen and stretch this way and that to suit your purpose. The following shapes, called *templates*, are available in most graphics programs:

► Rectangles and rounded rectangles

► Circles and ovals

► Polygons and regular polygons

You still use the basic two-point system. For example, if you want to draw a rectangle, choose the rectangle tool from the Tools menu. Then hold down the mouse button where you want the upper-left corner of the rectangle to start. Drag the mouse to where you want the lower-right corner of the rectangle to end, release the button, and there is an instant rectangle.

If you need to change the size of the shape later, move the cursor to one of the edges, hold down the mouse button, and stretch the shape to whatever size you need.

You can center your shape on-screen by stretching the shape out from a center position rather than from an edge. This gives you more control over where the shape appears on-screen.

130

To center the shape, choose Draw Centered from the Options menu or enter the center command. Hold down the mouse button at the place where you want the shape centered, and drag the mouse until the shape is the size you want. The sides of the shape are drawn at an equal distance from the center.

Manipulating Shapes

Once you have some basic shapes on-screen, you can start moving and modifying those shapes to construct more complex illustrations.

Selecting a Shape

You can select a shape or a portion of an illustration in much the same way that you select a block of text with a word processor. Mark the image you want to modify or use, and then enter a command, telling the program what to do with the image.

Mark the image by choosing the selection tool from the Tools menu, clicking the mouse button to the upper left of the image, dragging the mouse to the lower right of the image, and clicking again. The selection tool draws a loop or lasso around the image.

Some programs offer a simpler method of selection. After you choose the selection tool, just move the cursor anywhere inside the object and click the mouse button to select it. You can then decide what to do with it—move it, reduce or enlarge it, or even lay it on top of another image.

Moving and Stacking Shapes

Once you've selected a shape, you can move the shape across the screen. Position the cursor inside the shape you want to move, hold down the mouse button, and drag the shape anywhere on-screen (see Figure 8-3).

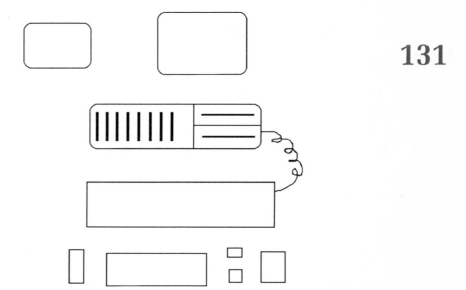

131

Figure 8-3. Moving shapes.

You can then rearrange the separate parts without having to redraw them. Although moving a shape across the screen isn't much of a feature by itself, when it's combined with a stacking feature, it gives you a pretty powerful tool. With it you can stack basic shapes one on top of another to create recognizable objects, (see Figure 8-4).

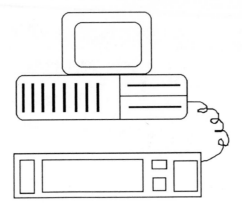

Figure 8-4. Stacking shapes to create objects.

132 *Rotating Objects*

If you draw an object but it's just not in the right position, rotate the object to make any necessary adjustments with the rotating tool.

Select the object you want to turn, choose the rotating tool from the Tools menu, then pivot the object around its center point until it's in the required position.

Erasing Mistakes

To erase something on-screen, select the eraser tool from the Tools menu. Hold down the mouse button and drag the mouse over whatever you want to delete. It's as easy as erasing chalk off a blackboard!

Zooming In

If your drawing is a little too detailed to edit, use the zoom feature to zoom in for a close-up view. Select the portion you want to view, and enter the zoom command. When you've finished editing that portion of the text, zoom out again to see the big picture.

Some programs offer zoom features that let you add or erase pixels one at a time (see Figure 8-5).

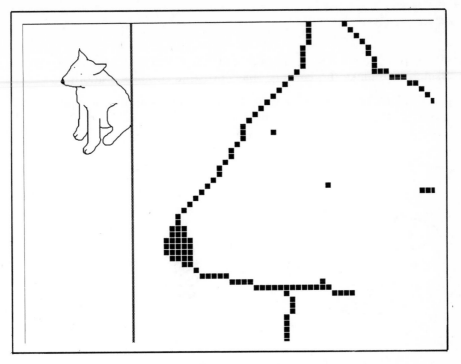

Figure 8-5. Erasing pixels one at a time.

133

Enhancing Your Drawings

Once you've finished your basic sketch, *and saved it to disk*, you can begin to add enhancements to perfect the drawing.

> ▶ **Tip:** If you're just playing around to see what looks good, don't save the changes to disk. By adding your enhancements in RAM only, you can abort your changes and return to the original at any time.

Shading

Most programs offer at least some basic method of shading your sketches to make the various objects distinct from one another.

Select the object you want to shade, and choose the pattern you want to use. The program automatically fills the selected object with the specified pattern (see Figure 8-6).

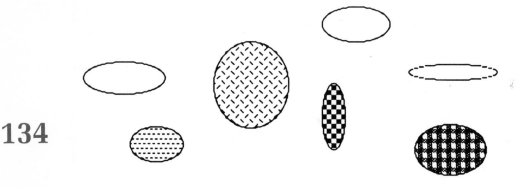

134

Figure 8-6. Objects shaded with various patterns.

If you want more complex shading to give objects a three-dimensional look, consider buying a program with one of the following paint tools.

The Spraypaint Tool

The spraypaint tool acts as an air brush, spraying pixels on your screen. You can adjust the width of the spray as well as the pattern of spray to modify the shading.

When you choose the spraypaint tool from the Tools menu, the cursor turns into a small circle of spraypaint. Hold down the mouse button and drag the mouse wherever you want the paint to appear. Drag the mouse faster for a thinner ribbon of paint or slower to lay down more pixels in a given area. When you first use the spraypaint tool, play around with moving the cursor at different speeds or paint in different patterns. When you've finished spraying, let up on the mouse button.

The Brush Tool

The only difference between the brush and spraypaint tools is that the brush cursor is a little smaller and the line thickness does not vary according to the speed of the mouse. You choose the brush thickness the same way you would choose line thickness for the line tool.

Smoothing the Rough Edges

When you're drawing lines on-screen, you'll notice that the edges get kind of sharp. It's just not that easy to bend a line on-screen.

To overcome this weakness of draw programs, many offer a feature that smooths the rough edges and rounds the sharp corners, making your illustrations seem as though they've been drawn by hand.

135

Adding Labels and Notes

Although draw programs weren't designed to handle huge blocks of text, you can add labels and draw arrows to point out important areas of the illustration.

Simply choose the text tool from the Tools menu, position the cursor where you want to enter the label, and start typing. MacDraw II even lets you add a white background to whatever you type to keep it from getting lost in the shaded areas.

> ▶ **Tip:** Be careful with the text. Most draw programs handle text as graphics elements, making the text very difficult to edit. The process may require you to cut a portion of the text and paste in a revised portion. Aligning the revised text can be extremely frustrating.

Saving and Reusing Sketches

One of the main reasons that graphics programs are so popular is that they let you create a file of sketches that you can use to create other sketches. Such a file of previously-drawn art is called clip-art. You may, for example, spend a great deal of time drawing a hand or a particular machine. If you then need to use that same hand in the same position in another sketch, you'd have to do some fancy tracing. If you need a blowup of a certain part of the machine, you'd have to enlarge that section and trace it.

With computer graphics, you can store all of these sketches in a file and call up the file when you need to use a particular sketch. If you need a blowup, select a section of the sketch, erase everything outside the lasso, and enlarge what's in the lasso. If you need to include a hand in your sketch—one that you drew in the past—call it up and plop it down in the new sketch.

136

> ▶ **Tip:** Saving your sketches to disk results in an additional benefit. Because the original sketch is stored safely on disk, you can call up the original, play around with it as much as you like on-screen, and then simply erase (undo) the screen without making any changes to the original.

Beyond the Basics

Now that you've seen all the basic features, let's look at some of the advanced applications for computer graphics.

Computer Transparencies

Computer transparencies let you draw complete sketches or sections of sketches on separate screens and stack the sketches to create new drawings or to focus on a part of the drawing. If you've ever seen transparencies used effectively, you know how powerful they are at illustrating the selected detail of a particular sketch, especially a complex sketch in which the detail could get lost.

With computer transparencies, you can include as much detail as you want for one particular aspect of the sketch without losing any details. Work on one part of the sketch at a time, perfect the details, and lay those details on top of the previous layer.

If you want a complete picture, including all the detail, simply stack the transparencies. Do you want to highlight one aspect of the sketch? Lay that transparency on top or remove the others.

Using Scanned Photos and Figures

If you have a photograph or a drawing on paper, and if you have the right equipment, you can turn your existing photos into pixel versions. You need a *digitizer* or a *scanner* that converts the image into a series of dots and stores it on a disk. Once the image is in your system, you can edit it as any other sketch (see Chapter 9).

137

Computer-Aided Design and Manufacturing (CAD/CAM)

As you've seen, computer graphics alone is a pretty amazing breakthrough. But coupled with advances in robotics technology, computers have single-handedly revolutionized industry.

With computer-aided design, engineers can design and test a part to determine any faults or weaknesses . . . before they even make one!

When they finally decide to manufacture the part, they can simply write a program that uses the dimensions in the drawing to specify how the part is to be machined. The program tells the machine just how to move the tool to cut the part to the specified dimensions.

Although a machine operator may need to adjust the program to account for some variations, once the program is set up, the machine can manufacture one identical part after another, hour after hour, without suffering from fatigue.

What You've Learned

Graphics programs are fun. When you first get the program, start playing. Because these programs are visually oriented, you need to get a feel for moving the cursor and modifying the basic shapes. While you experiment, keep the following points in mind:

▶ With graphics programs, you can create basic line drawings for flow charts, schematics, and other flat art, as well as for more intricate designs.

▶ If you're going to use graphics programs for most of your work, equip your system with a high-quality printer and a mouse or similar tool.

▶ Graphics programs give you a wide range of tools that let you create, manipulate, and enhance your illustrations.

138

▶ With the selection tool, you can choose a sketch or part of a sketch and move, modify, or rotate that sketch to suit your needs.

▶ Before you begin experimenting with a sketch, save it to disk so that you can go back to the original if you make a mistake.

▶ You can assemble several basic sketches to form a single complex sketch or to enlarge a portion of a sketch to use as a blowout.

▶ Computer transparencies let you layer sheets of detail over a basic outline.

Chapter 9

Desktop Publishing

In This Chapter

▶ *Designing and printing your own illustrated newsletters, brochures, and books*

▶ *Adding graphics to the page*

▶ *Previewing pages*

▶ *Special DTP hardware*

▶ *Do you need a DTP?*

Just a few years ago, you had to enlist the help of a graphic artist and a typesetter to bring your brochure or newsletter concepts to life on the printed page. You spent hours designing the pages, making sure you left enough room for the sketches, and writing instructions for the typesetter. Then you had to sit down with an artist and explain every sketch and what you were trying to illustrate.

When all the parts were finished, you faced the tiresome task of pasting down the pages and any sketches that needed to be inserted. If you made a mistake or wanted to experiment with alternative layouts, you had to cut and paste, always anticipating the effects of the change on surrounding text and pages. And for each change you wanted to make, you had to pay the typesetter dearly.

With desktop publishing, you don't have to guess how a certain font or typestyle will look on a page—you see it on-screen. You can try different layouts to fit the space you have to fill. Of course, desktop publishing programs can't give you artistic talent, or a flair for page design, but they do give you complete control over your page, letting you arrange and rearrange until the page is just the way you like it.

Understanding Desktop Publishing

Desktop publishing programs are really designed to work *with* word processing (see Chapter 5) and graphics programs (see Chapter 8). The word processing program creates the text, the graphics program creates the graphics, and the desktop publisher combines them together on a page (see Figure 9-1). You can use a desktop publishing program as your only program, but if you want the full power that word processing and graphics programs offer, you should use the three programs together.

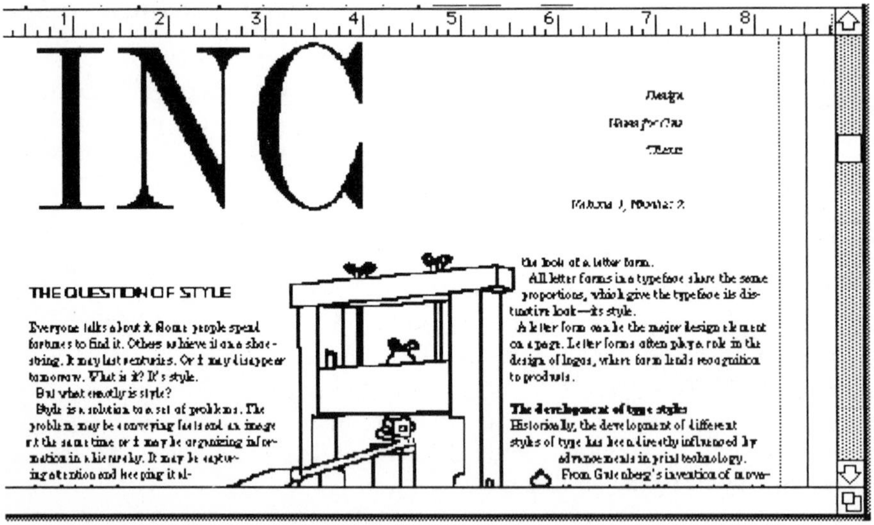

140

Figure 9-1. Desktop publishing integrates word processing and graphics.

This basic structure gives rise to the command structure within the desktop publishing program: text commands, graphics commands, and page layout commands.

Designing the Text

Remember, text commands let you experiment with the appearance and spacing of the characters on a page. Most desktop publishing programs offer a variety of type styles or enhancements that you can use to emphasize a word or phrase. Use the styles sparingly, however. Several different styles on a page may make a nice poster, but it'll detract from the content. Most programs usually offer the following styles:

Plain — This is the default, the same as having no enhancement.

Bold — Bold adds emphasis. Use bold to introduce important points, such as **Note:** or **Tip:**, or for section headings. Use bold sparingly or it loses its impact.

Italic — Italic isn't used to set off key phrases or words. Because italic isn't as strong as bold print, it's usually safer to use.

Outline — Outline provides an outline around the character. It's a fancier enhancement, used for cards, newsletter headlines, and announcements.

Shadow — Shadow shades around the base of characters to give them a three-dimensional look. This is another fancy enhancement that makes the characters look more like graphic elements.

Condense — Condense prints tiny characters. This is an excellent choice for footnotes or other text that you want to include without detracting from the main text.

Overstrike — Overstrike is a lot like bold, except that it gives your letter a double-image look.

141

In Chapter 5, we introduced fonts, sets of characters that share a typeface and point size. The following are examples of fonts:

Century Schoolbook 18-point
OCR/B 10-point
Helvetica 12-point
Times 9-point

You can use various fonts for titles and headings, to set off special elements (such as tables) from the rest of the text, or to emphasize a block of text.

> ⊘ **Warning:** When using different fonts, make sure that your printer can print them; otherwise, the font will appear on-screen, but it won't be printed.

All letters are defined by four guidelines: the *baseline*, *x-height*, *ascender*, and *descender*. (See Figure 9-2.) The baseline is an imaginary line on which text rests. For most purposes, you want text to appear on the baseline, although special characters such as subscripts and superscripts appear elsewhere. The x-height is the vertical space filled by lowercase letters. An ascender is the part of a letter that sticks above the x-height and a descender is the part that hangs below the baseline.

142

Figure 9-2. Basic type anatomy.

Extra space, called *leading*, is inserted between each line of type to keep the characters from reaching into the lines above and below. The more leading you have, the farther apart the lines of text. Leading is measured in points and is usually added to the type size to determine a spacing from baseline to baseline. For example, if you're using a type size of 10 you may want to add two points of leading between each line. Your baseline-to-baseline measurement would be 12 points (10-point type + 2-point leading).

Kerning means reducing the space between individual characters. Without kerning, certain letters within words may look uneven—some characters may be far apart while others nearly overlap. Kerning lets you adjust letter spacing so your words look attractive, especially for large type sizes such as headlines

▶ **Tip:** Remember, justification aligns blocks of text in relation to the left and right margins. Normally, text is left-justified—that is, *flush* (aligned) left with the left margin with a *ragged right* margin. To right-justify the text, spread it out so that it's flush with both left and right margins. To center-justify the text, move it to an equal distance between the margins. Figure 9-3 shows how the different justifications look.

This is an example of left-justification. Notice how the left side of the paragraph aligns but the right side of the paragraph looks jagged?

Left justification

This is an example of right-justification. Notice how the right side of the paragraph aligns but the left side of the paragraph looks jagged?

Right justification

143

This is an example of center justification. Notice how each line of the paragraph appears centered but the left and right sides appear jagged?

Center justification

Figure 9-3. Three ways to position text.

Hyphenating Words

Desktop publishing programs offer a hyphenation feature that automatically hyphenates a word if it runs past the right margin. You're given several options in using this feature:

▶ Turn off hyphenation, so words are not automatically hyphenated

▶ Specify how to hyphenate specific words

▶ Specify certain words that you don't want hyphenated

► Specify the maximum number of consecutive lines that may end in a hyphen

► Specify the minimum number of characters in a word to hyphenate—if you set this value to 5, the program does not hyphenate any words containing five characters or less

Automating the Design with Stylesheets

Chapter 5 discussed stylesheets, a neat way to set up specifications for typeface, point size, typestyle, indentation, and justification.

Importing Text

144

Although you can create text directly in a desktop publishing program, you may save time by creating the document first with your word processing program. You can then copy the file to your desktop publishing program to begin designing it.

Most desktop publishing programs can use files created by the more popular word processing programs—WordPerfect, Microsoft Word, WordStar, and MacWrite. If you are using a less popular program, you can save the document as an ASCII file or use special file conversion programs, such as those discussed in Chapter 4.

Adding Graphics

Most desktop publishing programs include some basic features that let you draw sketches and move graphic images on a page. For example, you can paste a graphic image in the middle of a page and desktop publishing programs provide a wrap-around feature that lets text *flow* around a graphic image. Text may either wrap around the artificial boundary of the graphic image, or around the graphic image itself (see Figure 9-4).

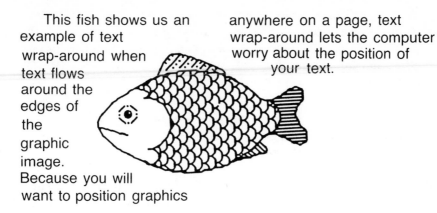

This fish shows us an example of text wrap-around when text flows around the edges of the graphic image. Because you will want to position graphics anywhere on a page, text wrap-around lets the computer worry about the position of your text.

Figure 9-4. Text wrap-around.

Graphics commands are excellent for using and modifying sketches created in graphics programs, but they usually don't offer the flexibility of a full-featured graphics program. Because desktop publishing programs don't offer the complete range of tools that a full-featured graphics program offers, you may want to create your sketches with the graphics program and then *import* it into the desktop publisher.

145

Most desktop publishing programs can use graphic images stored in popular file formats such as MacPaint, MacDraw, Lotus 1-2-3, and PC Paintbrush.

▶ **Tip:** If you write a letter using a popular program, such as WordPerfect or WordStar, and create a graph using Lotus 1-2-3 or Harvard Graphics, you can copy these files into the desktop publishing program and start working with them. But if you use a less popular word processor or graphics program, the desktop publishing program may not be able to use the files. You need a file converter program, such as those discussed in Chapter 4, that converts the files created in one program to files that can be used in another program. When you're out shopping, make sure the converter programs you buy perform the conversions you require.

As an added option, many programs include a *screen-capturing* feature. If you created a graphic image using another program, a screen-capturing program lets you copy the image directly to a file format that the desktop publishing program can use.

Laying Out Pages

Page layout commands define margins, columns, and the placement of text and graphics. The first time you lay out a page for a particular publication, you need to invest some time designing the page and specifying the settings. But once the design is perfected, you can save it as a template. The next time you need to print a similar page, use the template instead of re-creating the design.

146

The Page Size Setting

The first thing you do is specify the size of paper on which you intend to print. (Make sure it's a size that your printer can handle.) Most programs let you choose from a list of five standard page sizes:

▶US Letter (8.5 by 11 inches)
▶US Legal (8.5 by 14 inches)
▶Tabloid (11 by 17 inches)
▶A4 Letter (8.27 by 11.69 inches)
▶B5 Letter (6.93 by 9.84 inches)

Previewing a Page

Because you're making pages, you'll want to see what the whole page looks like as you're designing it—how the graphics images look in context, how the headings appear in their different fonts, and how any text enhancements appear. The page preview feature lets you check all these elements *before* you print the page.

Although most computer screens can display only half of a page at a time, desktop publishing programs offer the following page preview options:

Half Size lets you see what the entire page looks like, using half the screen; use this option to see how facing pages look.

75% Size lets you see a larger version of the entire page.

Actual Size lets you see what the entire page looks like—reveals more detail than the 75% view.

Double Size lets you focus on the detail of the page. You can use this view to preview fonts and type styles.

You could also buy a program that tricks your computer into thinking that the screen is larger than it really is. A screen enlarger lets you scroll through your pages quickly. Without a screen enlarger, your computer will redraw your pages each time you scroll up or down, forcing you to wait.

Locking Objects in Place

Once you've placed an object on a page, you may want to lock it into place so you can't move it or modify it by mistake. The desktop publisher offers a lock feature that lets you do just that.

If you lock an object in place and want to move it later, unlock the object first. This is most useful when you're creating pages for newsletters or brochures in which certain items, such as titles and headlines, must remain fixed.

Fine-Tuning the Layout

Master pages let you create text or graphics that you want to appear on every page, such as page numbers, titles, and running heads. If you do not want to use the text or graphics from a master page, you can turn it off for certain pages.

A *grid* divides a page into columns and rows, letting you align text and graphics precisely on a page. Many programs also include a *snap to* feature. When you move text or graphics on the grid, the snap to feature snaps the object to the nearest grid line for consistent alignment.

To help you align text and graphics on a page, desktop publishing programs may have horizontal and vertical rulers, displaying inches, centimeters, or picas.

Special Desktop Publishing Features

What separates one desktop publishing program from another are the number and type of features it offers. Some programs are great for designing single pages for brochures and newsletters, but they just don't offer the comprehensive features required for publishing long documents that contain repetitive page layouts, like books.

When looking at different programs, decide what types of publications you need to produce. If you're a casual user, programs like PFS: First Publisher offer enough basic features to get the job done without overwhelming you with complexity.

For more intensive work, a program like PageMaker or Ready,Set,Go! provides more features for refining the appearance of your pages. If you need to work exclusively with desktop publishing, look at programs such as Ventura Publisher, Quark XPress, or DesignStudio that offer special features for publishing, such as the ability to rotate text on a page, modify shading in digitized images, or revise graphics without degradation in resolution.

148

Desktop Publishing Equipment

Desktop publishing programs can work on any type of computer, but you can buy special hardware and software designed to simplify the task and make the program easier to handle.

Special hardware includes fancy printers that make your page appear more attractive, full-page monitors that display entire pages of text at a reasonable size, *optical mice* and *trackballs* that let you move the cursor with ease, and digitizers that give you the power to lift images or text from paper and insert it into your document.

Laser Printers

You can use a dot-matrix printer to print your pages, but most simply cannot give you professional quality.

If you don't want the quality lost in the printing, use a laser printer. You can buy two types of laser printer—a PostScript or a non-PostScript. Figure 9-5 shows a comparison of the output from each.

Non-PostScript costs less but may print certain fonts or graphics with jagged edges. For pages that use simple graphics such as bar graphs or pie graphs, a non-PostScript printer will be the most economical to buy. The most popular non-PostScript laser printers are made by Hewlett-Packard.

PostScript costs more, but is essential if you intend to print complicated graphics and a wide range of fonts. The most popular PostScript laser printers are the Apple LaserWriters made by Apple Computer.

PostScript prints the curves of letters smoothly.

149

Non-PostScript prints characters with noticeable jagged edges.

Figure 9-5. Printouts from a non-PostScript and a PostScript printer.

Full-Page Monitors

Most computer screens can display only part of a page at a time; you need to scroll the page to see the rest of it. That's fine for editing text, but when you're designing pages, you need to see the entire page at once.

To see a full page on-screen, you need a single or dual page monitor. As their names suggest, a single page monitor lets you see one page at a time, whereas a dual page monitor lets you view two pages side by side, letting you preview the facing pages of a manuscript.

Mechanical and Optical Mice

Because much of your work in the desktop publishing program consists of moving blocks of text and graphics and modifying graphics, you should have a mouse to move the cursor with ease.

Although many people use a mechanical mouse that rolls on a table top, optical mice have proven more popular because of their precision. When you move a mechanical mouse, the cursor movement can be affected by dirt on the tabletop, or by the mouse sliding instead of rolling. An optical mouse, however, uses a grid that detects the motion of the mouse.

For more control over cursor movement, you can calibrate the mouse to move the cursor slower for more precise movements or faster to move the cursor in leaps and bounds across the screen.

150

Digitizers

You don't need to rely entirely on sketches from your graphics program to illustrate your text. Sometimes, you'll want to include a photograph or pre-existing drawing that's not stored in a file. To do this, you need a digitizer or a scanner.

A digitizer converts images into a series of dots and stores them in a file. Once the image has been saved, you can modify it as if you had drawn the image with the computer. Depending on the types of images you need to scan, you can use either a *hand-held* or *flatbed digitizer.*

Hand-held digitizers are best for scanning small pictures or unusual shapes. Because these digitizers usually offer poor scanning resolution, they are not very good for scanning detailed images like blueprints. A flatbed digitizer is great for scanning detailed images. They resemble photocopying machines. You place the image face down on top of the digitizer, which scans the image and stores it in a file.

Many digitizers can also scan in text with special *optical character recognition (OCR)* software. These programs can scan printed material, such as magazine or newspaper articles, and convert them into ASCII files that you can edit using a word processor.

File Converters

Since desktop publishing programs act as managing editors, they're designed especially to work with different word processors and graphics programs. You simply import the text and graphics from other programs into the desktop publisher.

Screen Capturers

At times, you may want to include an image that appears on your computer screen in one of your documents. You could photograph your computer screen and scan it in the computer using a digitizer, but the resolution would be poor, and the process would be time consuming. An easier solution is to use a special screen capturing program that takes a snapshot of your screen.

151

A screen capturing program stores a screen image in a disk file. Then you can print the file and paste it in your document by hand, or you can import the file in your desktop publishing program. Once you have copied the image in the desktop publisher, you can edit it like any other graphic image.

Screen capturing programs can be essential in many cases. Many of the illustrations in this book were created using a screen capturing program. Without them, we would have had to photograph the screens.

Do You Need a Desktop Publisher?

All these fancy desktop publisher features give you a lot of control over page design if you're combining large chunks of text with several graphics elements. However, if you're working mostly with graphics and just a little text or mostly with text and a smattering of graphics, you may not need the extra control that the desktop publisher offers. You may be able to get by with a word processing program that offers basic graphics or a graphics program that lets you type small chunks of text.

The Word Processor Alternative

If you don't want to invest the time and money learning to use a desktop publishing program, try a full-featured word processing program. Many word processors now support several fonts and typestyles, let you preview pages, and offer basic graphics features that let you draw flow charts and schematics. For more complex sketches, you can draw them by hand, label them on the typewriter, paste them in place, and copy the page.

Of course, there are some drawbacks. For one, most word processors are capable of creating only basic sketches and will not let you move or modify graphics elements easily. Another problem is that many programs let you import graphics from another program, but they can't display those graphics on-screen so you can edit them. They only display a shaded area so you can see where the graphic image will appear and how it affects surrounding text.

152

The Graphics Program Alternative

If you use the computer primarily to draw sketches and to type a few chunks of text to accent the art, you don't really need the services of a desktop publisher. Graphics programs offer commands and tools that the desktop publisher cannot equal, such as the ability to rotate graphic images and change their sizes.

Graphics programs give you the freedom to insert text, but they treat text as graphics, making it very difficult to edit. You cannot import text from another file, so you need to type the text on the same page as the graphic image. If you need to edit text, you must erase it, just as you would erase a line, and then type the correction. It's clumsy, but if you're only typing labels or captions, you don't really need that much control over the text.

What You've Learned

If you need to create professional-looking publications on a regular basis, or if the thought of controlling the publication of your own newsletters and brochures intrigues you, desktop publishing is for you. You will enjoy the freedom it gives you in playing with the page, and you'll appreciate the time and money saved in corrections alone. Before you move on, review some of the main points about desktop publishing:

▶ Desktop publishing programs combine text and graphics from other programs to form fully illustrated pages.

▶ Although desktop publishing programs do let you type text and create graphic images, their main purpose is to manage the text and graphics that are created in the full-featured word processing and graphics programs.

▶ The preview feature lets you review the page design before you print a page on paper.

▶ Many word processors provide basic desktop publishing features, supporting several fonts and letting you create basic graphic images.

▶ Dot-matrix printers can be an inexpensive way to print your pages, but laser printers produce a more professional look.

▶ Stylesheets let you save your page design and format so you can use it again.

▶ Master pages let you create text and graphics to appear on every page of a document.

▶ Digitizers can scan both text and graphics into your computer.

▶ Full-page monitors can display an entire page on the screen at once.

153

Chapter 10

Talking to Other Computers

In This Chapter

▶ *Using modems to send and receive files and programs through telephone lines*

▶ *Sharing and accessing information through electronic bulletin boards and on-line databases*

▶ *Using your modem to try out software programs for free*

▶ *Tips for telemarketing*

Telecommunications lets you connect your computer to any other computer in the world. You can then share information, pictures, or even entire programs with that computer.

With the proper telecommunications software, you can retrieve data from another computer, make airline reservations, shop, leave and answer messages, and even play games with someone clear across the country. And that's not all—read on.

The Universal Network

The process of telecommunications works by converting information into electrical impulses for transmitting over telephone lines. The computer, receiving these impulses, converts them back into usable information again. Since you can convert any information into electrical impulses—text, numbers, or graphics—you can send any type of information to any other computer around the world.

Bulletin Board System (BBS)

A Bulletin Board System (BBS) enables your computer to answer the phone when other computers call. By using special BBS software, other people can copy files to and from your hard disk, leave messages, and play games stored on your computer.

156

Many people set up a BBS for fun, but many businesses (especially computer dealers and software publishers) have set up electronic bulletin boards for their customers to use to leave suggestions or complaints. If several branches of a particular company need to share information, a BBS can help them keep up-to-date on the latest news and breakthroughs. Some software publishing companies set up a BBS to advertise new products or to sell products that are not available at local stores.

Remote Computing

Remote computing lets you control another computer anywhere in the world—Miami, Paris, Bangkok. You sit at your computer but you harness the power, programs, and information from the other computer for your own use.

Popular remote computing programs, such as Carbon Copy and PC Anywhere, give you the freedom to work anywhere you want with whatever computer you're hooked into.

The biggest users of these remote computing programs are consultants. Instead of driving to a client's site, the consultant can call the client's computer. With both the client and the consultant sitting at their computers, the consultant can lead the client step-by-step through a program. If problems arise, the consultant can copy, delete, or modify files stored on the client's computer, fixing the problem immediately.

Telegaming

Many games let you play against a real live opponent—no matter how far away—rather than against the opponent furnished by the program. As long as you each have a copy of the same game, you can play chess, checkers, backgammon, or arcade games with your computers through the phone lines.

For board games such as chess, both of you will see the exact same screen and can watch each other. For arcade games such as jet fighting or tank dueling, each person's computer shows a different point of view, making the fight as realistic as possible. You're controlling an F-16 jet fighter while your archenemy is flying a MIG-23. As each of you manipulates your jet, you must respond to the other's moves. Strategy, counterstrategy—you'll love it!

157

On-Line Databases

For a fee, you can subscribe to an on-line database such as Compu-Serve, the Dow Jones News Retrieval, or Prodigy. An on-line database provides files as does an electronic bulletin board, but may also let you buy and sell stocks, shop, make travel reservations, and access encyclopedias, newspapers, or magazine articles from around the world.

Getting Started

First, you need to physically connect your computer to another computer. You can do that in either of two ways:

▶ Through a serial or null modem cable

▶ Through modems attached to both computers and to a telephone line

Once the computers are physically connected, you need a software program that tells your computer how to send and receive data from another computer.

Null Modem Cables

A null modem cable connects the *serial ports* of the two computers. This method is used most frequently for sharing files among several computers in a single office; this is called *Local Area Network (LAN)*.

A LAN connects a group of computers that are usually located in the same room or building. Many companies have IBM, Macintosh, and mainframe computers connected so someone using a Macintosh can send a file to the mainframe or IBM computer.

LANs have more uses than just transferring files, however. LANs also let a group of computers share equipment. Rather than buy a printer, modem, or hard disk for each computer, a group of computers can share them. Since not everyone will need to use a printer or modem all the time, sharing equipment through a LAN eliminates the need and expense of buying additional equipment.

To use the LAN, each computer must use special networking software that acts like a traffic cop, making sure information flows smoothly between computers. For connecting large numbers of computers, many LANs require each computer to have a special networking board plugged inside along with special networking software. The latter controls the network and the former physically connects each computer to the network.

Some networks have a special computer that does nothing but keep the network running. This computer, called a *file server*, is usually the fastest computer on the network. Without a file server, the network may not work or it may work slowly because every computer on the network may be trying to send information simultaneously. A file server simply makes sure that every computer has a chance to send and receive information.

One of the most popular uses for networks is sharing files, especially database files. Without a network, each computer may need a separate copy of a database file. If two computers add information to their separate copies, neither copy will be complete. Eventually the problem occurs when you have multiple copies of the same database file, yet none of them contain the exact same information.

158

Networks prevent this problem by storing a single database file on one computer. When other people need to use or update it, they can access the file through the network. Any changes they make will affect that one file. Thus the problem of keeping multiple copies of a database file is eliminated.

The null modem cable can also be used to transfer files from a laptop computer that uses 3 1/2-inch disks to a desktop computer that uses 5 1/4-inch disks and to transfer files between different computers, such as an IBM and a Macintosh.

Modems

Remember, a modem lets your computer send and receive data through the telephone lines. Any telephone line will work, although people who use a modem frequently find it convenient to dedicate a whole phone line to it so they can still place regular calls while the modem is sending and receiving. Modems even let two different types of computers communicate. A person in Atlanta can use an IBM compatible computer to call a Macintosh computer in Los Angeles, as long as each computer is connected to a modem (see Figure 10-1).

159

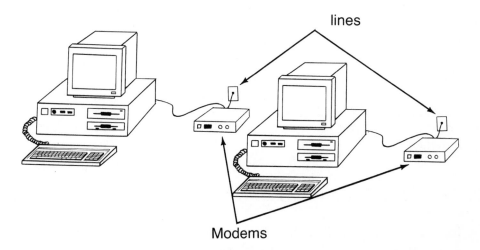

Figure 10-1. A modem lets computers communicate by sending signals over telephone lines.

The criteria for choosing a modem rest on

▶ how rapidly it transmits electrical impulses
▶ whether it's internal or external
▶ and whether it is Hayes-compatible.

An internal modem is connected through the computer's expansion slot, making it a part of the computer. The external modem connects to the serial port of the computer and sits next to the computer like any other peripheral device.

Internal modems take up less space because they are housed inside the computer. They are especially useful if you're using the modem with a laptop computer; you won't have an additional box to lug around.

160

An external modem is best if you plan on using it for several different computers. You can unplug the external modem and connect it to any computer—IBM PC, Macintosh, Commodore 64, or Cray XP-48 supercomputer.

The *Hayes modem*, made by a company called Hayes Technologies, has set the standard in the modem market. Because of its popularity, most communications programs are written exclusively for the Hayes modem. When you're shopping for a modem, make sure it offers Hayes compatibility; otherwise, you may not be able to use many programs.

A Hayes modem understands certain commands, called the AT command set. To test if you have properly connected a Hayes-compatible modem to your computer, load your telecommunications program, type AT, and press Enter. If you see the message OK, you have connected your modem properly. If you have not, typing AT has no effect.

Telecommunications Software

In addition to a modem (the hardware), you must have a telecommunications program (the software) installed in your computer before you can start talking with the world. Both computers must have this software installed, although it need not be the same software. A Macintosh computer in Boston may be using White Knight while an IBM in Chicago is using ProComm Plus; they'll understand each other.

Some modems come packaged with communications programs, but most of the time you need to buy one of the following four types

▶ Dedicated communications programs
▶ Communications programs in integrated packages
▶ Communications programs in desktop organizer programs
▶ File-transferring programs

Dedicated here means that the program is set up exclusively for communications via modem. Since the program is dedicated to tele-communications, it can offer several advanced features that the more general programs can't afford to offer. We look at some of these features later in this chapter.

If you're planning to use the modem frequently to access or share information, you should consider purchasing one of the dedicated programs: CrossTalk, ProComm Plus, or White Knight.

161

An integrated package, such as Microsoft Works or PFS: First Choice, is a single program that contains the capabilities of a word processor, spreadsheet, database, and telecommunications program.

Because an integrated package contains so many features, the features of each portion tend to be limited. For example, the word processor portion of an integrated package does not offer all the features of dedicated word processors like WordPerfect. Likewise, the telecommunications portion of an integrated package offers fewer features than dedicated telecommunications programs like Crosstalk.

At the very least, the telecommunications program in an integrated package lets you call other computers, send and receive information, and receive calls from other computers. However, an integrated package may lack features like a dialing directory, different transmission protocols, or script files.

Desktop organizer programs often provide several utilities, such as a notepad, calculator, calendar, and communications program. Like integrated packages, the communications programs found in desktop organizers provide the necessary features to call another computer and transfer information, but they don't offer many advanced features. Some popular desktop organizers are Sidekick Plus, Lotus Metro, and PC Tools Deluxe.

File-transferring programs work with null modem cables to connect computers without using the phone lines. If you need to connect several computers in one office, even if they're different types of computers, you'll need a null modem cable and a file-transferring program to do the job. Usually, both are included in a single package.

The package may also include a cable to connect the computers through their *parallel ports*. This is preferable to connecting to the serial ports because parallel ports can transfer data much faster. (That's why most printers connect to the parallel port.)

If you need to transfer files between a Macintosh and an IBM, or between an IBM desktop computer and an IBM laptop computer, a file-transferring program is much easier to use than an ordinary telecommunications program.

With the latter, you need to define the communication parameters (such as baud rate) on both computers and you need a telecommunications program for each computer. In addition, you may need to convert files from one format to another. If you wrote a letter on a Macintosh using MacWrite, you first have to convert the file to a format that an IBM computer and word processor can understand. With a file-transferring program, the process is much simpler. It comes with two versions of the program, one for each computer. Thus, the process of defining communication parameters is much simpler.

162

A file-transferring program also may automatically convert files. Some popular file-transferring programs are LapLink III, LapLink-Mac, and MacLink Plus.

Dialing Direct

Now that you're all hooked up, you're ready to start calling these other computers and transferring data. To dial a number using most communications programs, you just type **ATDT** (for touch tone) or **ATDP** (for rotary) and then the number you want to dial, for example, **ATDT 619-555-1234**.

Once you have the other computer on the phone, you perform either of two activities. If you want to transfer information from your computer to the other computer, you *upload*. If you want to get information from the other computer, you *download*. Each communications program has its own commands for uploading or downloading.

Special Features

Although the procedure for using a modem is fairly basic, many dedicated communications programs offer special features, including

▶ Dialing directory

▶ Auto-redial

▶ Background processing

▶ Script files

▶ Log files

▶ Terminal emulation

▶ Transmission protocol

A *dialing directory*, as shown in Figure 10-2, lets you store your most frequently called phone numbers. Rather than typing the entire phone number, the computer dials it for you.

163

```
            D I A L I N G     D I R E C T O R Y

           Name              Number      Baud P D S  E   CMD File
      1- ProConm Support BBS   1 314 449-9401   2400-N-8-1  N
      2- ComputorEdge On-Line  1 619 573-1675   1200-N-8-1  N
      3- Rasta Think Tank      1 619 282-1211   2400-N-8-1  N
      4- Knowledge Works       1 619 528-1058   1200-N-8-1  N
      5- PC Magnet             1 800 346-3247   1200-N-8-1  N
      6- .....................   . ... ...-....   1200-N-8-1  N
      7- .....................   . ... ...-....   1200-N-8-1  N
      8- .....................   . ... ...-....   1200-N-8-1  N
      9- .....................   . ... ...-....   1200-N-8-1  N
     10- .....................   . ... ...-....   1200-N-8-1  N

    ==>        R Revise      M Manual Dialing      Entry to Dial
               P LD Codes    D Delete Entry        F Find
               PgUp/PgDn Page L Print Entries      ↑/↓ Scroll
               Home Top Page  End Bottom Page      ESC Exit

    Modem Dial Cmd: ATDT              LD Codes Active:
    Dial Cmd Suffix: !               Com Port Active: COM1

                         AUTO DIALER
```

Figure 10-2. The dialing directory.

Busy signals can stop even the most advanced computer from reaching another computer by telephone. To prevent you from having to redial the same phone number repeatedly, many communications programs provide an auto-redial feature. If the communications program dials a number that's busy, the program hangs up the phone and tries again until it gets through. When the computer finally gets through the line, it beeps to let you know.

Many communications programs include a *background process-ing* feature that lets you use your computer while it's busy dialing. The moment the program gets through, it beeps to let you know. Then you can exit the program you are working on and start using the communications program.

When you call another computer, you usually must enter a password and identification number before the computer will give you access to its information. Since these steps can be time-consuming and repetitive, some programs let you create a *script file* that types the commands for you.

164

> ► **Tip:** Besides automating the process of dialing another computer, script files can also operate your computer in your absence. A script file lets you leave your computer and modem turned on, and then at a certain time, the script file can call another computer, upload or download information, and hang up. Since phone rates are cheapest during the nights and early morning hours, script files let you take advantage of these lower phone rates without having to stay up all night yourself.

To create a script file, you need to know which keys you press at any given time. You could record your keystrokes on a piece of paper as you type your commands, but it would be a lot easier if your computer could record your commands for you.

Log files do just that, storing your keystrokes in a separate ASCII or text file so you can review them later and turn them into a script file. You can also use a log file to capture any messages that the other computer displays on your screen. That way if the messages scroll by too fast or if want to review the messages later, you can retrieve the log file and review whatever you wish.

Larger computers, such as mini and mainframe computers, only work with certain types of computers or terminals, so even if you can link up with one of these computers via modem, you may not be able to transfer information.

To help you deal with this problem, many communications programs provide *terminal emulation*. This lets your personal computer mimic a computer or terminal that the mini or mainframe computer will recognize.

Once you have connected two computers together, you can type messages on your screen and send them to the screen of another computer. If you want to send data stored in files to the other computer, however, you need to use a *transmission protocol*.

A transmission protocol is a specific method for sending files between computers. When transferring data, both computers must use the same transmission protocol in order for the transfer to be successful. The following three are the most common.

> *ASCII Protocol* is the simplest, but it has two drawbacks. It can only send ASCII (text) files, not program files, and it does not check the integrity of a file as it is sent or received. If the telephone line has static, the static could damage a file. Because this protocol doesn't check for the integrity of the file, neither the sender nor the receiver can be sure that the file is good.
>
> *XModem Protocol* solves the problems inherent in the ASCII protocol. You can transfer any type of files, and during transfer, the XModem protocol checks the file integrity, ensuring that the file you sent or received is intact. Essentially, the XModem protocol sends a file in chunks or packets of information, each packet containing 128K of data. It then waits for the other computer to acknowledge that it received the package. If the amount of information the receiving computer got doesn't match the amount sent, the sending computer sends the same packet of data again.
>
> *YModem Protocol* works the same as the XModem protocol, except that the YModem protocol sends data in 1,024K packets of data instead of 128K. Hence, it's much faster.

165

Communication Settings

Besides using the same transmission protocols and running at the same baud rate, telecommunications programs must also use the same communication settings—*parity*, *data bits*, and *stop bits*—in order for the transfer to be successful.

The parity bit is used to check a unit of data for errors during transmission. Common parity bit settings are None, Odd, and Even. Data bits are used for storing information. Common data bit settings are 7 and 8. Stop bits mark the end of data. Common stop bits are 1 or 2.

Before you begin using your modem, you need to specify these settings in a communications setup screen, like the one shown in Figure 10-3.

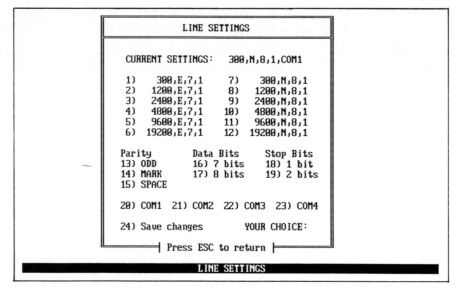

Figure 10-3. A communications setup screen.

Tricks and Traps
of Telecommunications

As you've seen, telecommunications lets you share messages, data, and programs with other computers around the world. Because of this, you have access to several special services that provide free programs, software updates, and other important products and services. But you have to be careful. When you open your doors to this vast world of information, your computer becomes vulnerable to certain problems called Trojan horse or virus programs.

Using Programs on a Trial Basis

Most of the programs introduced in this book, such as WordPerfect and Lotus 1-2-3, are *commercial* programs. That is, you go to your friendly neighborhood computer store, purchase the program, and start using it. You don't really know if the program will meet your every need until after you pay for it.

Shareware programs work the opposite way. You copy the shareware program through your modem and use the program on a trial basis. If you like it, send a registration fee to the publisher. In return, you will receive the latest version of the program along with a printed manual and a phone number to call for help.

If you don't like the program, give it to someone else or erase the disk. Unlike commercial programs which rely on stores for distribution, shareware programs rely on a network of computers and users to distribute and advertise the product. It's a good way to see what's new in the computer industry.

Some mail-order companies specialize in selling shareware programs. If you want to buy one, ask these companies for their catalog.

167

Getting Programs for Free

Unlike shareware or commercial programs, you can legally copy and use some types of programs for free. These are referred to as *public domain* programs, and they are usually very simple and rarely accompanied by manuals.

Some examples of shareware programs are: PC-Write, a word processor that offers nearly as many features as top-rated programs like WordPerfect and Microsoft Word; AsEasyAs, a spreadsheet that works like Lotus 1-2-3; and PC-Outline, an outlining program that rivals commercial outlining programs like ThinkTank.

Public domain programs are usually simple programs that don't require detailed instructions. Some popular public domain programs for IBM computers are WhereIs, a file searching program; Silence, a program that turns off the speaker in your computer; and QuicKeys, a program that speeds up the movement of your cursor.

Trojan Horse and Virus Programs

Trojan horse and virus programs are designed to ruin your hard disk by erasing or damaging your files. A Trojan horse program disguises itself as a useful program, such as a game or word processor, but when you run it, the program displays flashy graphics to keep you occupied while it erases your hard disk.

Virus programs are trickier. A virus "infects" an existing program file and waits for a certain condition to occur, such as April 1 or Friday the 13th. Until that condition occurs, the virus keeps "infecting" files on every floppy disk you use in your computer. When April 1 or Friday the 13th appears, the virus attacks, wiping out your hard disk files.

If you've made backup copies of your hard disk files, you can copy your backup files to your hard disk. Unfortunately, the virus may have infected your backup disks, which means the virus can erase your hard disk all over again.

168

> ▶ **Tip:** The best way to protect yourself against a virus or Trojan horse is to keep up-to-date copies of your hard disk files, and to write-protect your program disks as soon as you get them home from the store. Recall that write protecting lets the program be read, but will not allow anything to be written on the disk, including a virus (see Chapter 4).
>
> The virus can only infect program files, not the data files that you create, so do not copy any program files from your hard disk. By copying only data files, you ensure that you do not copy a virus to your backup disks.
>
> For additional safety, you can buy antivirus programs or diagnostic software that will help you find and destroy the virus. For more information, refer to Chapter 14 on Computer Security and Maintenance.

Cutting Down on the Phone Bills

The more files you transfer between computers and the larger the files, the more expensive your phone bill is. To cut costs, you can transfer files in the middle of the night using script files, as discussed previously.

Another way of saving money is to condense the files you want to send, by using an *archiving program*. Archiving programs compress several files into one and tighten up individual files. This lets your computer send the same amount of information a lot faster, saving you money.

What You've Learned

Telecommunications gives you access to information and programs from various sources throughout the country and around the world—and it's all as easy as making a phone call. When you begin using your computer to communicate with the world, keep the following information in mind:

169

- ▶ Bulletin board systems (BBSs) let other people call your computer to leave messages, transfer files, or play games.
- ▶ Remote computing lets you use another computer as if you were physically at the other computer's location.
- ▶ Telecommunications programs may be part of an integrated package or a desktop organizer program, but they probably won't offer as many special features as a dedicated program.
- ▶ To transfer files between a laptop and desktop computer, or between an IBM and a Macintosh, you can buy special file-transferring programs such as LapLink.
- ▶ Communications programs offer features like a dialing directory, auto-redial, and script files to automate the process of calling another computer.
- ▶ Terminal emulation lets your computer mimic the features of another computer so you can connect to a mini or mainframe computer.
- ▶ Transmission protocols let you transfer files between two computers. Each computer must use the same transmission protocol to do this.
- ▶ Public domain programs are those you can legally use for free. Shareware programs are those you can use but are legally obligated to buy if you continue using them.
- ▶ Archiving programs can lower your phone bill by reducing the number and size of the files you want to transfer.

Chapter 11

Writing Your
Own Programs

In This Chapter

▶ *What computer programming is all about*
▶ *Why it's helpful to learn programming*
▶ *The basic steps required to program any computer*
▶ *Getting started*
▶ *Choosing a programming language to learn*

How much you need to learn about programming computers depends on what kind of work you'll be doing. If you're simply using the computer to perform common tasks, you can find plenty of programs on the market to fill your needs.

On the other hand, you may want to perform a complex, unusual job requiring a special program that you can't find on the market. If that's the case, you need to hire a consultant or learn to write your own programs. Even if you choose the former, it helps to know how to program so you can modify what the consultant designs for you. You might get in a pinch and have to perform a quick fix to meet a deadline. Besides, programming is fun!

You can break the programming process down into four basic steps —two that deal with actual programming, and two that deal with follow-up activities:

▶ Plan what you want the program to do, and what steps will lead to the desired outcome.

▶ Write the program in a language that the computer can understand.

▶ Test the program to make sure it works as planned.

▶ Write documentation for the program, so others can learn how to use it.

Planning the Program

The hardest part about programming is thinking in a logical, step-by-step manner. Before you even sit down at the computer, make a list of what you want the program to do, and what steps lead to the desired result.

If you want to write a program that calculates the average of five numbers, your plan might look something like this:

1. Have the user type in five numbers.
2. Add the five numbers together.
3. Divide the total by five.
4. Print the result on the screen.

You've already seen that a computer needs software to perform its tasks. It also needs some list of instructions that tell it exactly what to do. Programming consists of writing sets of these instructions. Each set is written in a particular *language*.

Instructions consist of very basic, long lists of commands. You must think of every command ahead of time and anticipate all the possible ways the computer might misunderstand it. In other words, you have to anticipate problems and remember all the details.

All programs must contain the following four types of commands:

▶ Input
▶ Storage
▶ Operations
▶ Output

Input

Every program begins by prompting the user to enter some information—words, numbers, names, addresses, whatever. The program must display a menu, a message, or a signal of some sort, asking the user to type certain information. One of the first commands in any program asks for input.

For example, if you were writing a simple BASIC program on an IBM computer, you might enter the command

```
10 PRINT "Enter five numbers"
```

to have the computer display a message that asks you to enter five numbers. Let's look at this command in a little more detail:

> *10* sets the sequence of commands. Why 10 instead of 1? The zero is tacked on to leave space for additional commands that you might want to add later: 11, 12, 13, etc.
>
> *PRINT* is a BASIC command (BASIC is a programming language). It tells the computer to print to the screen whatever is typed next.
>
> *"Enter five numbers"* signals the program to print to the screen exactly what's between the quotes.

173

Storage

Your program must have some way to store information temporarily so the program can work with it. It must have some system of reference, a system that assigns a variable to each piece of information you enter.

The following program is a continuation of the one started earlier. The five numbers are assigned to the variables A, B, C, D, and E:

```
10 PRINT "Enter five numbers."

20 INPUT A, B, C, D, E
```

Notice that the line starts with the number 20 and the BASIC Input command.

Operations

Now that the computer has some information to work with, you can start entering commands to tell it what to do with the information. The following commands build on the previous two, telling the program to add the five numbers and then divide the total by 5 to determine the average:

```
10 PRINT "Enter five numbers."
20 INPUT A, B, C, D, E
30 TOTAL = (A + B + C + D + E)
40 AVERAGE = TOTAL/5
```

Output

To show the results of your program, the program must output these results. You need to add a command at the end of your program, telling it to supply the output. You can direct the output to the printer, the screen, or to another computer. The following command was added at the end of the previous commands, telling the computer to print the resulting average to screen:

```
10 PRINT "Enter five numbers."
20 INPUT A, B, C, D, E
30 TOTAL = (A + B + C + D + E)
40 AVERAGE = TOTAL / 5
50 PRINT "The average is", AVERAGE
```

Programming Languages

Computers only understand commands as a series of electrical impulses. By stringing together lists of impulses and gaps between impulses, you generate a command that makes the computer perform some practical task.

Because these strings of electrical impulses are difficult to understand and manipulate, various programming languages have been developed to help you program in English and to provide a shorthand for developing more coherent instructions.

Simplicity isn't the only goal—languages also attempt to be as versatile as possible, so that one command can perform a variety of tasks, depending on the context. With a versatile language, you can combine the commands in various configurations to perform a wider range of tasks.

Machine Code

The most basic programming language consists of two numbers—0 and 1—that represent the presence and absence of an electrical impulse. The language is known as *binary code* or *machine code*. A string of these codes might look like this:

```
0001 1101 0101 0110
1101 0100 1111 1001
1001 1000 0010 0101
```

175

As you can see, working with a language that describes electrical impulses can result in some burdensome, incoherent programs. Hardly the simple commands we saw earlier!

Assembly Language

Assembly language is one step up from machine code. It condenses multiple machine code instructions into simpler instructions such as MOV, JMP, or ADD. Although a single instruction to print a message might take several pages of instructions in machine code, a similar program in assembly language might consist of the following instructions:

```
DOSSEG
.MODEL SMALL
.STACK 100h
.DATA
SayHello DB 'Hello, World!', 13, 10, '$'
.CODE
mov ax,@Data
mov ds,ax
```

```
mov ah, 9
mov dx, OFFSET SayHello
int 21h
mov ah, 4ch
int 21h
END
```

As you can see, the instructions are a little easier to understand; ADD means to add two numbers, MOV tells the computer to move data, and JMP tells the computer to jump to a different instruction.

This still isn't the best, however. Assembly language requires several instructions to perform even a simple task such as multiplying two numbers, or in the previous example, to print "Hello World!" on the screen.

176 *High-Level Languages*

Since machine code is so difficult to understand and manipulate, and since assembly language is so bulky, most programmers use *high-level languages* that are easier to write and understand. These languages provide a shorthand system that combines many of the codes into a simple command that's easy to understand. You may have heard of the common ones: FORTRAN, COBOL, BASIC (which we saw earlier), Pascal, C, and Ada.

A high-level language uses instructions that resemble English. For example, the following BASIC program waits for you to type your name and then it prints it on the screen.

```
10 PRINT "Enter your name"
20 INPUT A$
30 Print "Hello,";A$
```

High-level languages have the additional advantage of *portability*; that means that you can run them on different computers. To translate a program written in a high-level language into machine code, you need a compiler.

Which Language to Learn?

The language you should learn depends on what you want to do. If you want total control over your computer, you should invest your time learning assembly language.

The problem is that this power comes at a price. As you saw above, the language is bulky and difficult to understand. If you're just starting to learn about computers, you may want to avoid assembly for a while.

Since machine code and assembly are so difficult to understand and manage, most people learn a high-level language, such as BASIC, C, or Pascal instead. BASIC and Pascal were designed especially for beginners; they offer sensible commands, moderate power, and a good deal of versatility. Since IBM and compatible computers come with BASIC, this is a good language to start out with. But if you want a little more power and some added features, Pascal is a good choice.

177

If you're looking for still more power, you might benefit by learning a more complex language, such as C. C is a fairly simple language that gives you more flexibility than either Pascal or BASIC. The same commands that might take three or four instructions in Pascal or BASIC can be achieved with one instruction in C. For example, compare the following two programs:

```
1 PROGRAM Pascal;              1 main () /* PROGRAM C */
2 VAR                          2    {
3   I : byte;                  3    int i;
4 BEGIN                        4    for (i = 0; i < 10; i++)
5   I := 0;                    5      {
6   FOR I < 10 DO              6      /* Do something here */
7     BEGIN                    7      }
8       (* DO something here *) 8   }
9       I := I + 1;
10    END;
11 END. (* PROGRAM Pascal *)
```

They are functionally equal, but notice how the C program requires fewer instructions compared to the Pascal program.

If you just want to experiment with programming, learn BASIC. If you plan to write complicated programs for distribution, consider

BASIC, Pascal, C, Modula-2, or Ada. You can write any program in any language; the only difference is that some languages may be easier to use for certain tasks than others.

Getting Started

In order to start writing programs, you need two essential programs and one optional program, as shown in Figure 11-1:

▶ An editor

▶ A compiler or interpreter

▶ A debugger (optional but helpful)

178

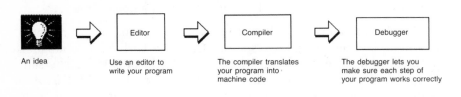

Figure 11-1. How the editor, compiler, and debugger work with you to create a program.

An *editor* lets you write the actual program. If you don't have a special programming editor, you can use any word processing program instead.

Compilers and Interpreters

Once you've written your program, you need to convert it to machine code so that the computer can understand the program and run it. There are two types of conversion programs: compilers (called *assemblers* when used for assembly language programs) and *interpreters*.

Generally, compilers are more useful than interpreters, because they let you use your program on a wider range of computers. Since the compiler translates your program into the universal machine code, other computers don't need a copy of your compiler to run the program, and since the program is stored in the more cryptic machine code, it's more difficult for others to figure out how you wrote the program. If you plan on sharing your program or selling it to people who use different computers, you should use a compiler.

Interpreters translate your program into machine code every time you run it. Therefore, anyone who wants to use the program must have a copy of your interpreter. That makes it a little tougher to sell the program.

And since the program is written in a clear, understandable language, it's easy for anyone to see how the program is written and pirate your secrets. If you're trying to sell your program, that could hurt.

Debuggers

Once you've written a program, you need to test whether it works correctly. Since a program may contain several hundred instructions, the chance of making a mistake is extremely high. To help you find any bugs in a program, you need a debugger, a special program that lets you see the results of your program instructions, step by step, for better or worse. Then you can go back and work the bugs out. You're looking for three types of errors:

Syntax errors occur when you misspell a language command. For example, if you typed the print command as PRINTT instead of PRINT, you would have a syntax error—the command would not work. With GW-BASIC, the moment you type a command that will not work, the language program displays an error message.

Logic errors occur when the program does perform a task but not the task you wanted. A logic error in the previous example might occur if the program divided the total of five numbers by four instead of five. This would print the wrong answer, but as far as the computer is concerned, the program is working fine. To troubleshoot for logic errors you need to run each command in your program, step by step, and examine the result. The moment something goes wrong, you will know exactly which command is to blame.

Run-time errors are tough to find. With them, the program works most of the time, but if you press the wrong key, the program fails. With syntax errors, your program won't even work. With logic errors, the program works but gives the wrong answers. With Run-time errors, the glitch is unpredictable. You may not know there's a problem until after you've sold the program or shared it with your colleagues.

180

▶ **Tip:** To test a program for run-time errors, you have to play dummy. Type any and every possible combination of keystrokes that an unwary user might mistakenly type while using the program. You can also give the program to a test group of users, and have them try to mess it up.

Debugging any program can be extremely difficult and tedious. Because of this, most programmers divide programs into parts called *subprograms*, *procedures*, or *functions*. By dividing a program into smaller parts, you can isolate possible problems quickly and perform the required fix. Once you have thoroughly tested and debugged a subprogram, you never need to debug it again.

The Flow Chart

Sometimes you want the computer to proceed with one set of instructions if a certain condition holds true or with another set of instructions if the condition is false. You need to set up some Yes-Or-No questions, so that the computer can decide how to proceed. A good way to begin is to construct a flow chart, like the one in Figure 11-2.

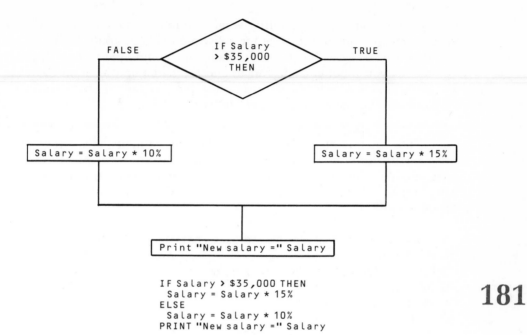

```
IF Salary > $35,000 THEN
   Salary = Salary * 15%
ELSE
   Salary = Salary * 10%
PRINT "New salary =" Salary
```

181

Figure 11-2. A flow chart.

If you can translate the tasks you want to perform into these flow charts, you've won half the battle. It's difficult at first, but after you've programmed for some time, you'll start to think like this.

Once you have a flow chart thought out or written up, all you have to do is start expressing the various commands in whatever programming language you choose. When you've written a list of commands that performs a specific task, you've succeeded in writing a program. You can store the program on disk and play it back just as you can with any commercial program.

Providing Instructions for the User

Getting a program to work can be cause for celebration, but as you're pouring the champagne, don't forget to write instructions for the users, and for yourself.

Programs are always familiar when you're in there grappling with each command, but put it aside for a few months and you'll likely forget it. Write down what each program and subprogram does, what commands you must enter to run it, and the name and location of the program. That way, when you want to use the program or try to update it, you have thorough records that you can understand.

You can also keep records on how your program works by adding comments directly in the program. Adding comments to a program does not affect the way a program works, but lets you explain what the program does. For example, the following comment was written for the sample program we wrote. Note that the BASIC command for adding a message is REM:

```
 5 REM Averages five numbers-Date Last Modified: 2/15/90
10 PRINT "Enter five numbers."
15 REM Wait for user to type in five numbers.
20 INPUT A, B, C, D, E
30 TOTAL = (A + B + C + D + E)
40 AVERAGE = TOTAL / 5
50 PRINT "The average is", AVERAGE
60 REM *** End of program. ***
```

182

What You've Learned

After reading this chapter, you should have a clearer idea of what programming is all about. If you're interested in learning more about programming, Howard W. Sams & Company offers a full line of books to get you started. For now, review some of what you learned in this chapter:

▶ A computer program consists of instructions that tell the computer what to do, written in a language it can understand.

▶ A program contains four types of commands: Input, Storage, Operations, and Output.

▶ Machine code (binary code) is the most basic programming language; it describes the electrical impulses that make up a command.

▶ Assembly language condenses multiple machine code instructions into simpler instructions.

▶ High-level languages simplify programming by packaging several machine codes in a single command and assigning a name to the command that's easy to understand.

▶ Compilers convert a program into machine codes and store these machine codes on disk.

▶ Interpreters convert a program into machine codes and store these machine codes in the computer's RAM.

▶ Programming languages differ in the number of instructions you need to perform a specific task and in the number of ways you can use specific program instructions.

▶ BASIC and Pascal are programming languages that were designed especially for beginners. More advanced programs, such as C, give you more control over the computer's operations.

183

Chapter 12

Finding the Right Computer for You

In This Chapter

▶ *A stroll down computer row—what's on the market and what makes some computers better than others*

▶ *Evaluating your computer needs*

▶ *Finding a less expensive computer that does the same job as its expensive counterpart*

▶ *Desktop, portable, and laptop computers*

▶ *Reading between the lines of computer advertisements*

▶ *Local dealers vs. ordering by mail*

We would like to tell you what the best computer is—what's the best buy for your money—but that's simply impossible. There are so many good computers on the market and so many variables, that we cannot give you any hard and fast criteria to use when shopping for one computer.

What we can do, however, is tell you how to decide what's best for you. We can tell you some of the common mistakes that many people make when shopping for computers and some of the tactics used by salespeople to dump obsolete equipment on unwary shoppers. Once you know what to watch for, you'll be able to avoid the more common pitfalls and save a little money in the process.

Choose the Right Brand

As you get more and more involved in the world of computers, you'll quickly learn how dynamic the computer industry can be. Software publishers continually update their programs with new features, and hardware manufacturers design new, faster computers that can run this improved software more efficiently. Users band together and share information in order to keep up with the changes. That's why it's so important, especially when you're first starting out, to buy a popular computer—a computer that others can help you learn.

186

If you buy an IBM or Macintosh computer, you'll be able to find all sorts of software, books, newsletters, users groups, repair centers, and any other support that you need to help you learn and develop your skills. You'll be able to trade data simply by swapping disks with people. You can even use customized programs that other people develop. Buy a less popular computer, and you'll find that the resources are few. The money you save won't begin to pay for the frustration you'll encounter.

The Simplicity of a Macintosh

If this is your first computer, if you're planning on getting a computer for your office that's easy for everyone to learn, or if you need to do a lot of graphics, consider a Macintosh. One style is shown in Figure 12-1.

Figure 12-1. The Macintosh SE/30.

The Macintosh computer is completely menu-driven and includes a mouse, making it easy to start using with very little instruction. If you need help, most of the programs offer context-sensitive help screens that explain everything you need to know.

There are several types of Macs from which to choose; your choice will depend on your budget and on what software you want to run. The Macintosh Plus and Macintosh SE are less expensive, but the Mac Plus may not be able to run some of the newer programs, and the SE is not as expandable as the newer Macintosh II computer. Either one of these models may meet your immediate requirements, but may limit your future goals.

The more expensive versions—the Macintosh IIci, IIcx, IIfx, and IIx models—are more flexible. If these do not meet your future requirements, you can install *expansion boards* that give the computer more memory and power.

The Power and Speed of the IBM   187

If you're looking for the most popular and inexpensive computers, consider buying an IBM or IBM compatible computer, as shown in Figure 12-2. Since IBMs and much of their software are command-driven, you'll find them a little more difficult to learn than the Macintosh. But once you learn the commands, you don't have to work your way through menu after menu to perform a task.

The newer IBMs support the mouse, and many IBM programs are designed to work with or without the mouse. If you plan on doing graphics, make sure the computer you buy supports a mouse.

Figure 12-2. The IBM PS/2 Model 80 features a floorstanding unit.

IBM no longer makes the PC/XT or AT models, so if you're buying a new computer, you won't find these. But if you're looking for a used computer, you should be aware that these older models are still floating around. Unfortunately, the PC/XT cannot run the latest programs because it is too slow, does not have enough memory, and cannot display color graphics. This computer is fine for recreational or home use, but if you plan on using it for business, get something more powerful.

The IBM AT computer overcomes the limitations of the PC/XT by running faster, offering more memory, and displaying color graphics.

The IBM PS/2 computers come in Models 25, 30, 50, 60, 70, and 80. Models 25 and 30 are similar to the IBM PC/XT computers, which means they're slow and don't have enough memory to run many programs. For the price, Models 25 and 30 offer few advantages over IBM compatible computers discussed in the next section.

188 The PS/2 50 and 60 computers are more like the IBM AT. If you need speed, consider the PS/2 70 and 80 computers that use the more advanced 80386 microprocessor.

Getting More for Your Buck with IBM Compatibles

IBM compatible computers work exactly like IBMs, except that many compatibles are faster, cost less, and use higher quality parts than their IBM counterparts. You may have heard of some of the better known IBM compatible computers, including Compaq, AST Premium, Dell Computers, Northgate, ALR, Zenith, Hyundai, Everex, and Epson.

Compatibility refers to both hardware and software. Software compatibility means you can run IBM software on the compatible computer without any problems. Hardware compatibility means you can use IBM parts to repair and upgrade your compatible.

Although the compatibles have a lot to offer, you need to be a little more careful when shopping for compatibles. Don't look only at the price tag; consider compatibility as well. If you go with a well-known compatible, such as Compaq or Dell, it is not a problem, but with some lesser-known brands, you may not be able to run certain programs, and you may have trouble finding equipment that works with the computer. If you're considering buying a compatible, ask the sales person for phone numbers of people or businesses who have been using that model. Check with them to see if they've had any problems.

Taking a Risk with IBM Clones

The word *clone* is a derogatory term describing a computer assembled by a local computer dealer. Clone computers have the same status as generic food—they cost less, but may not offer the same quality as the name-brand compatibles. We say *may not* because some clones are actually superior to their name-brand counterparts. Quality varies, depending on who's making the particular clone.

The biggest problem you may have with a clone is getting the dealer to honor your warranty. If you buy a name-brand computer such as Compaq or Epson, you can take your computer to an authorized dealer in any city in America and they will honor your warranty and be able to fix your computer. With a clone, your warranty is only good as long as you live near the dealer and as long as the dealer stays in business. If the computer needs repair, you may have the additional task of finding a competent and reliable technician to fix it.

189

The Unique Benefits of Other Computers

Although Macintosh and IBM are the giants of the computer world, there are several other computers out there.

The Commodore Amiga is great for displaying on-screen graphics. It can display more colors at a higher resolution than either the Macintosh or IBM. If you need to store and display digitized photographs on screen, the Commodore Amiga is the computer of choice. By adding the appropriate expansion boards, you can make the Amiga use IBM software.

Unfortunately, the Amiga does not have a large number or variety of programs available in comparison to the IBM or Macintosh. If you need a word processor or database with special features, you may have a hard time finding the program you need.

The Atari ST costs less than a Commodore Amiga, can display nearly as many colors, and can use both IBM and Macintosh software with the purchase of additional equipment. For those on a tight budget, the Atari ST offers the most computing power for your dollar. Like the Commodore Amiga, the number and variety of programs available for the Atari ST is much less than for IBM or Macintosh computers.

The Apple IIgs's main advantage is its ability to run Apple II software. Many schools use Apple II computers and software, so an Apple

IIgs is best for children because they can use the many educational programs available for the Apple II. If you're looking for a computer for home use, the Apple IIgs is a pretty good buy.

Choose a Computer for Your Lifestyle

Up to this point, you've seen the brands of computers available and the strengths and weaknesses of each. To add to the variety, some of the computers mentioned earlier come in three forms, depending on how mobile you need them to be: *desktop*, *portable*, and *laptop*.

The desktop computer is the most popular—and the bulkiest—of the three types. To reduce the amount of space a desktop computer uses, many computers advertise *small footprint* or *tower configuration*. A small footprint means that the computer is shorter in height or width at the sacrifice of fewer expansion slots or internal disk drive bays. Hence, these computers are usually less expensive than the standard desktop computers.

A tower configuration means that the computer is designed to stand upright underneath a desk. These computers usually cost more than their standard desktop relatives.

Portable computers come in two parts: a keyboard and a combination computer/monitor, as shown in Figure 12-3. "Portable" is used loosely here—a portable computer weighs anywhere from 20 to 30 pounds—but it's still more portable than a desktop computer.

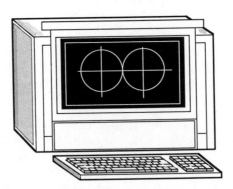

Figure 12-3. A typical portable computer.

The trouble with portable computers is that they're scaled-down versions of the desktop models. The monitor isn't quite as large or as good, many portables don't offer the same expansion capabilities, and you may get less memory. If you need to move the computer every week, or if you travel and do a great deal of work in hotel rooms, get a portable; you can use it wherever you can find an electrical outlet. If you move your computer only occasionally, you should stick with the desktop.

Most laptop computers weigh less than 12 pounds and run on batteries, so you can use the computer anywhere—in a hotel lobby, riding in a car or airplane, even on a boat! If you need to use a computer wherever you go, the laptop is for you (see Figure 12-4). However, you pay a price for this compact computer, both in money and in a loss of computer power. The least expensive laptops cost more than $2000, and that doesn't include a printer. The laptop offers less expansion capability than either the desktop or the portable, and its display can't come close to the resolution you can get on a standard monitor.

191

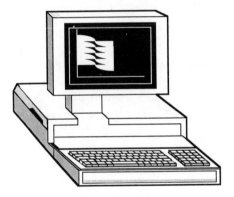

Figure 12-4. A laptop computer.

To overcome the poor quality of the display, many laptop computers offer *back-lit screens* that provide their own source of light or *gas plasma screens* that glow orange. If you need to display graphics on your laptop, determine the graphics standard that its screen can emulate: CGA, EGA, or VGA. If a screen only emulates CGA graphics but you need to run a program that requires EGA graphics, you won't be able to use the program on that particular laptop computer.

Before You Shop

When you begin shopping for a computer, you need to work backward. Figure out what you want to use the computer for now and what you plan on using it for next year. Think about what software you want to run, what operating system you intend to use, and what other hardware you want to connect to your system. Then, make sure that each piece of equipment you buy can work with the other pieces and the software you want to use.

Evaluating your computer needs may be the most difficult part of the shopping process because you must plan ahead. Although you'll do most of your software shopping after you buy your computer, you must know a few things about the software you intend to use; otherwise, the computer you buy may not be able to run the software (see Chapter 13).

192

When you know what software you want, read the label on the package and make a list of all of the hardware requirements for running each program. Your list might look something like this:

Computer required:	*IBM or compatibles*
Operating system:	*MS-DOS or PC DOS 3.2 or higher*
RAM required/desired:	*512K/640K*
Hard disk required:	*Yes*
Size of disks:	*5 1/4"*
Graphics required:	*Yes*
Monitor:	*Monochrome, CGA, VGA, and EGA*
Mouse required:	*Yes*

The computer stores only one program in RAM at a time, so you should look for a computer that has enough RAM to run your largest program. For example, if your accounting program requires 640K, you need a computer that has at least 640K RAM. The more RAM, the better; if you try to go cheap, you'll regret it later.

A good rule of thumb is to look for an IBM with 640K or a Macintosh with at least 2M RAM.

Next, determine how much storage capacity you'll need. Here's a step-by-step procedure you can follow to determine your needs.

1. Figure out how much memory your programs are going to use. For example, allow 2M for your operating system and other programs and 5M for a fairly large database program. So far, that's 7M total.

2. Determine how much information you want the disk to hold. For example, if you plan on storing 10,000 addresses, each consisting of 140 characters (including blank spaces), that's 1,400,000 characters (1.4 megabytes). That brings the total requirements to 8.4 megabytes.

3. Add a couple more megabytes for other documents you'll want to save, bringing the total to 10M.

4. Triple that figure to allow for future expansion. You need a 30M hard disk.

193

That's a good size and not very expensive. If you plan to use the computer for business, however, that may still be too little space.

▶ **Tip:** Remember every computer must have at least one floppy disk drive to run the programs you buy, and many of the newer computers feature two floppy drives, one of each size. However, although a hard disk is often optional, it's not worth doing without. (See Chapter 2 for a summary of disk drives.)

▶ **Tip:** Many programs are graphics-oriented; they can display a wide variety of fancy graphic images in various colors. If you want to get the most out of these programs, you need the specified monitor.

There are a few other items you should consider before you encounter your first computer sales person, including the microprocessor, *FCC certification class*, and expansion slots.

You may remember that the microprocessor is the computer's brain. It sets up and controls the communication network that is your computer. Processor names always appear as numbers, such as 80386 or 68030 and are often abbreviated, as in the phrase, "This baby's got a 286 with a 40 meg hard drive!" Get the most powerful processor you can afford—you won't regret it.

> ▶ **Tip:** The type and speed of the microprocessor is often included in the name of the computer—for example, a Northgate 286/16 has an 80286 microprocessor that operates at a maximum speed of 16 megahertz.

194

The Federal Communications Commission (FCC) rates computers by two classes, Class A or Class B, which indicate how much radio-frequency interference a computer emits. Class A means that you can safely use the computer in an office. Class B is a stricter rating that means the computer can be used in a home, where the chances of interfering with radios and televisions sets is greater. If you have a choice, go with Class B.

Every part of a computer plugs into a circuit board called the *motherboard*. The motherboard may contain up to twelve expansion slots that let you increase the capabilities of your system. You can then plug expansion boards (or cards) into the expansion slots, depending on your requirements. For example, if you buy a program that requires Hercules graphics, you can buy a Hercules graphics card that plugs into your motherboard.

When shopping for a computer, ask the dealer how many *open* expansion slots the computer has, not how many total expansion slots it has. Your computer might have eight expansion slots, but half of those slots are occupied by video boards (so you can use a monitor), disk drive controller boards (so you can use your floppy or hard drive), or memory boards (for RAM).

▶ **Tip:** Remember you can choose from three styles of keyboards (see Figure 12-5). Although they are arranged differently and the number of keys varies, there's not much difference between them—all can perform the required tasks. If you plan on typing a lot of numbers, however, get one with a separate keypad for cursor movement keys so you can use the numeric keypad solely for entering numbers.

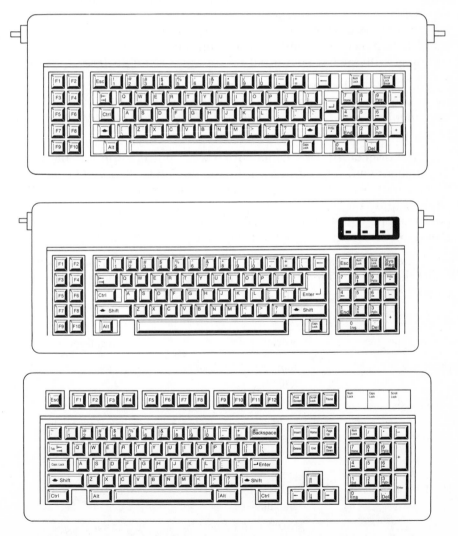

195

Figure 12-5. Examples of various computer keyboards.

Monitors, Power Supply, and Printers

You have two types of monitors from which to choose: color or mono-chrome; a color monitor displays color graphics. CGA monitors may cause eyestrain if used for word processing or other work that requires you to stare at the monitor all day. EGA and VGA monitors do not have this problem because they display higher resolutions.

Monochrome monitors can display characters and graphics in only one color, such as green or amber, but these monitors are less expensive and display sharper images than the color monitors. No matter which type of monitor you buy, the computer must have a video board to connect the monitor to the computer. Most computers come equipped with such a board, but be sure to ask the dealer.

Make sure the video board and monitor are of equally high quality. If you buy the cheapest video board possible and the most expensive monitor, you will only see what the cheap video board can produce.

The original IBM PC came with a weak power supply (63.5-watt); the moment you plugged in a hard disk, the power supply choked and burned out. Nowadays, nearly every computer comes with a better power supply ranging from 135-watt up to 220-watt. The stronger your power supply, the more expansion boards and disk drives you can plug into your computer without worrying about it burning out.

Chapter 2 presents basic information about printers and how to select the right one for your needs. Table 12-1 summarizes the pros and cons of each of the five types of printers.

Table 12-1. Choosing the Printer for Your Needs

Printer Type	Advantages	Disadvantages
Dot-matrix	Inexpensive, fast, prints graphics	Poor-quality printing
Daisywheel	High-quality printing	Slow, noisy, expensive, cannot print graphics
Thermal	Lightweight, battery-powered	Slow, poor-quality printing, requires special paper
Inkjet and plotters	Prints colors, prints graphics	Expensive
Laser	Excellent print quality, prints graphics	Expensive

A printer can make or break a computer system. No matter how beautiful documents and graphics look on-screen, if you have a lousy printer, everything's going to look lousy.

> ▶ **Tip:** Remember ports let you connect your computer to other equipment such as printers, modems, joysticks, or other computers. A computer may have several ports, but at the very least, every computer should have at least one parallel port and one serial port.

Although the modem is a small part of your computer, there's a lot to consider before you buy one. Table 12-2 summarizes the most important criteria you should use in making your decision:

Table 12-2. Modem Considerations

Feature	Recommendation
Speed	Speeds range from 1,200 baud up to 19,600 baud (not very common). Get a modem with a relatively high baud—2,400 or 9,600; otherwise, it'll spend a lot more time on the phone.
Internal/external	If you don't want the modem cluttering your desk, get an internal modem. If you want a modem that you can use on several different computers, purchase an external modem.
Hayes compatibility	Most telecommunications programs are written for Hayes modems. Make sure the modem you buy is Hayes-compatible; otherwise, you may not be able to run many programs.
Software included	Many modems come complete with the software required to run them. When comparing prices, be sure to take this into account.

> **Tip:** If you've decided to buy a laptop computer for working on the road, consider getting it equipped with an internal modem. That way, if you get stranded in the middle of nowhere without a printer, you can send your creations to your office and have your printer print them out.

Advertising Alert

198

When shopping for a computer, don't let computer advertisements mislead you. Many dealers artificially lower prices by considering such items as adequate memory, the keyboard, a monitor, or the operating system "extras."

An IBM or compatible computer should have at least 640K, and a Macintosh should have at least 2M; don't settle for less. To lower costs, dealers may advertise computers with less memory and then charge you extra for additional memory. When you're comparing prices, make sure you're comparing prices for the same amount of memory. If someone offers to sell you an IBM with 512K, ask them how much the additional 128K is going to cost you.

Some ads offer 512K of memory but are "expandable up to 1M on the motherboard." On the surface, this sounds like a great deal, but it usually means that the computer can *only* use 512K or 1M of memory.

For some odd reason, many computer dealers consider the keyboard an optional item. If you want a keyboard, you must pay extra for it. Is a steering wheel an optional item for your car? To determine the quality of a keyboard, feel the keys. If you can feel the letters, you can bet that they'll rub off in a short time. If the keys feel smooth, the letters have been bonded to the keys.

When you're looking at computer ads, don't just look at the pictures. The ad might show a computer with a color monitor, but that monitor is not included in the price or in the package.

Some dealers will sell you a computer, a printer, and a cable for connecting the two together, but when you get home you find that the port you need to plug the cable into doesn't exist. It's extra.

Some dealers include the cost of the operating system in the price that they quote you, others don't. You can't run the computer without one. If the computer does include an operating system, make sure it includes the documentation you need to learn the system.

Dealing with Dealers

Now it's time to go to the store, ask a lot of questions, take notes, and try out some of the computers on display. Make sure the salespeople can answer your questions. If they can't, go elsewhere.

Local Dealers

199

If you're a first-time computer shopper, the local dealer may be the best place to buy. You can try the computer in the store, the salesperson can help you make your decision, and the dealer can help you get started once you get the computer home.

It can also be the worst place to buy your first computer. Keep in mind that the dealer is trying to sell what's in stock. If an IBM compatible is the best computer for your needs and you walk into a Macintosh dealership, don't expect the salesperson to tell you that you really need an IBM. A few dealers are out to make a fast buck. They'll sell you the equipment, but they're not too keen on supporting you when you need help using it.

To find a dealer you can trust, ask your friends and colleagues for recommendations. Visit several dealers and ask the same questions.

The best dealer isn't necessarily the one with the lowest prices. Be sure the dealer offers the service you will need and can help direct you to the computer that's best for you.

Mail-Order Dealers

In the past, mail-order dealers had a bad reputation for selling mediocre equipment and for not delivering the goods, but that's changed. Mail-order firms have since established a strong reputation for quality and service rivaling that of local dealers, and at less cost.

You can find mail-order dealers through national magazines such as *PC Magazine* or *PC World*. (Apple Computers strictly regulates the price of its computers, so if you're looking for a deal on a Macintosh or Apple II, you may not find one.) Although mail-order dealers have improved their reputations, you should still check them out to make sure they're legitimate. You can use some of the following criteria as an acid test:

► Consistent advertising
► Toll-free number
► Credit
► Guarantees
► Support

200

Because full page advertisements in national magazines cost so much, look at several issues of the magazine to see which mail-order dealers can afford to advertise regularly. Make sure the company offers a toll-free phone number (or any phone number for that matter). Any mail-order company that can't afford a toll-free number most likely can't afford to give much support to its customers, and doesn't want to field complaints. The better mail-order dealers provide 24-hour, toll-free telephone support, 365 days of the year.

Call the dealer and find out how credit card orders are handled. The less reputable mail-order dealers will bill your credit card before they ship your product; that could be anywhere from one week to several months. The more reputable dealers bill your credit card on the day they actually ship your computer.

Because mail-order buying has the reputation for being risky, the better mail-order dealers offer 30 day money-back guarantees.

Some mail-order dealers have contracts with computer service sites in most major cities in America. If you know the exact part that's broken and your computer is still under warranty, just phone in your problem; the mail-order dealer will send you a new part and trust that you will return the old part in exchange.

Know Your Mail-Order Rights

Mail-order dealers must abide by the Federal Trade Commission (FTC) mail-order regulations which govern shipping delays, cancellations, and refunds. If you come across a company that does not abide by these rules, contact *Raymond Rhine, Room 4616, Federal Trade Commission, Washington, D.C., 20580, (202) 326-3768.*

Mail-order companies must ship products within 30 days of receiving payment, unless the company specifies a different amount of time in its advertisements. If a company cannot ship an item within 30 days, it must notify you and give you the choice to accept a refund or wait for another specified shipping date. If the company cannot specify a shipping date, it must explain why.

If a company cannot deliver a product by the new shipping date, the company must notify you in writing and set another shipping date.

If you do not agree to this new shipping date in writing, the company must cancel your order and refund your money. If you do not specifically request a refund, the company can legally assume that you accept the new shipping date.

Companies must send refund checks by first-class mail within seven days of cancellation. Credit card accounts must be credited within one billing cycle. Mail-order companies cannot issue credit vouchers in place of a refund. If you bought the items with a credit card and you're having trouble getting your refund, call your credit card company—they're good at getting money out of people.

201

Used Computers: Risky or Safe?

You'll find three types of used computers advertised in newspapers or local advertising weeklies: obsolete computers that someone wants to dump; nearly new, fully equipped computers; and some that are in between. With the first, the cost may be extremely low ($100 for a computer that retailed for $1,595 back in 1983), but because the computer is so old, it may be virtually useless for your purposes. If you're just starting out, avoid these deals.

The second type are sold by one-time owners who gave up trying to learn how to work them, and decided to try to get some of their money back. If you know exactly what you're looking for, you can get a great deal on practically new equipment. As a bonus, many people selling used computers tend to include software, furniture, and books as part of the deal. Take anything they offer—and make sure it's in good condition.

The third category includes computers owned by people who want to move up to a newer and/or more expensive computer. Some of these used computers may be "gently used," some may have been running every day for a year or two. Again, know what you want and learn as much as you can about what you're getting and who you're getting it from.

What You've Learned

Use this chapter as a framework on which to hang the additional information you'll gather from local dealers and from ads. To help you highlight some of the important points covered in this chapter, review the following list:

- ▶ Choose a popular brand of computer so that you can get the necessary support to learn and exploit its full potential.
- ▶ The Macintosh is one of the simplest computers to learn.
- ▶ Many IBM compatibles give you more power for your money, but if you want to play it safe, buy a genuine IBM.
- ▶ Clones are off-brand computers that offer a less expensive alternative to name-brand compatibles.
- ▶ Many name-brand computers offer portable or laptop models for greater mobility, but these computers may not offer as much power as the desktop models.
- ▶ Before deciding what kind of computer to buy, look at the software you want to run and evaluate your computer needs.
- ▶ Don't trust computer ads or sales pitches; if an ad sounds too good to be true, it probably is.
- ▶ Although used computers may be inexpensive, avoid them unless you know exactly what you're looking for.

Chapter 13

Smart Shopping for Software

In This Chapter   203

▶ *Evaluating your software needs*

▶ *Reading between the lines of software advertisements*

▶ *Evaluating software for free*

▶ *What to watch out for*

▶ *Locating specialized programs for solving unique problems*

▶ *Where to buy software at discounts of up to 60%*

You can find software for just about any task you want to perform from typing letters to managing a mortuary. You must know what's available, so you can find the best software product.

Once you know where to go to get the information you need, the rest is a matter of footwork and phone calls.

Step One: Determine the Type of Program You Need

Before you do anything, make a list of the types of programs you need. For example, you may need a word processor for writing letters and memos, a database for storing names and addresses, and a spreadsheet for doing your calculations. Table 13-1 gives a run-down of the various programs available.

Table 13-1. Choosing the Type of Program You Need

Software Type	Purpose
Communications	To transfer data with other computers
Database	To store names, addresses, inventory lists, and other information
Desktop publishing	To design and publish your own newsletters, brochures, and books
Languages	To write your own customized programs
Graphics	To create graphs from existing spreadsheet and database files and to draw your own pictures
Integrated	To perform the combined tasks of word processor, spreadsheet, database, communications, and graphics programs
Specialized	To solve unique problems such as office management, statistics, or inventory control
Spreadsheet	To perform calculations on financial, scientific, or numeric data (taxes, budgets, etc.)
Utilities	To provide convenient tools, to enhance the capabilities of your computer
Word processor	To write and type

Step Two: Compare Various Software Packages

Local dealers are the best source for information about the most popular software—what most people are buying, using, and returning. The only drawback with shopping through dealers is that they may not have the latest information; they're too busy trying to sell the programs they already have. As a result, you may get stuck with some outdated software.

Software Advertisements

The first place you should look for software is in magazines. Software advertisements provide the most timely information, sometimes advertising a product years before it hits the market. These ads tell you what's available and what will be coming out soon. In short, advertisements tell you two important things: what the program can do and who the competitors might be.

205

Advertisements list the main features of the program in the hope that some of these features will appeal to you. Examine the list closely; you may not have much need for many of the features and they can make the program more difficult to learn and use.

Advertisements may also compare a program to other programs and try to pummel the competition. Before you buy this "superior" software package, look at the other side of the story—the competitor's ad. If one program compares itself to another program, that's a good sign that the other program is worth considering.

Software Reviews

Look through magazines for reviews of the more popular software products. Although these reviews may be slightly dated, they do offer some sage advice that can prevent you from buying a program full of bugs.

The only problem with these reviews is that they're a lot like movie and book reviews—many are expressions of a particular writer's taste. So when you're reading reviews look past some of the information and see what the author has to say about the following criteria:

▶ Ease of use

▶ Speed

▶ Compatibility with other programs

Features that enhance a program's ease of use include tutorials, reference cards or keyboard templates, and context-sensitive help screens. If the program is menu-driven, it's a good bet that you'll find it easy to use.

Other factors that may influence ease of use are the clarity of the program manual, telephone support, and whether the program has any awkward features or commands that seem unnecessarily complicated.

Speed is a relative term. If you're shopping for a program that you intend to use for most of your work, look for a program that carries out your commands rapidly. It may be a little more difficult to learn, a little less helpful, but you can afford to spend time learning a program that will save you time in the future.

If you're going to be sharing information with several other users who may be using different programs, compatibility is an important consideration. Make sure the program uses and transfers data to the other programs you'll be using.

Step Three: Evaluate the Programs on Your List

Now you're ready to start narrowing down. First, read the hardware requirements on each software package on your list and throw out any programs that your computer cannot run.

Next, visit a local dealer and practice using the program on the dealer's computer. Of course, this isn't the most ideal setting in which to evaluate a program, but it will give you some idea of what the program looks like and how easy it is to learn.

If a local dealer doesn't carry the program that you want, or if you want more time to spend trying a program at your convenience, call the software publisher and ask for a demonstration disk.

Demonstration disks come in two types. The first type shows you how the program works but doesn't let you enter your own data. Since you can't experiment with the program on your own, you don't get the chance to see how easy or difficult the program is to use.

The second type of demonstration disk provides a limited version of the actual program. You'll be able to enter, print, and edit information, letting you see just how the program operates and some of the problems you'll encounter using it.

> ► **Tip:** When evaluating programs, use your instincts. If you don't like the colors, the way the program looks on the screen, or even the keys you must press to enter a command, cross that program off your list. If you don't like a program for any reason, you'll hesitate to use it and you may not be able to get the most out of it. No matter how many wonderful features the program offers, if you don't feel comfortable with it, it's not the one for you.

207

Step Four: Find the Best Price

Now that you know what you want, you can start thinking price, and that varies depending on where you do your shopping.

Local Software Dealers

The safest place to buy software is from a local dealer. Although these dealers carry only the most popular programs at the highest price, the price they charge is almost always less than the suggested retail price —usually 10% to 40% off.

For the modest markup, you do get some valuable services. The dealer will usually let you try out the program before you buy it and can answer any questions you might have right on the spot. If you have trouble with the program when you get it home, or if you just don't like it, you can return it for a full refund.

Mail-Order Software Dealers

Mail-order dealers offer a wider selection of software at less cost than local dealers. The prices usually range from 20% to 60% off retail price. Because these companies don't have to pay sales tax on out-of-state shipments, they pass the savings on to you. You can find these dealers through national magazines such as *PC Magazine* or *PC World*.

Before you buy software through the mail, check out the company according to the following criteria:

▶ Consistent advertising
▶ Toll-free number
▶ Credit
▶ Guarantees

208

Look at several issues of these magazines to see which mail-order dealers advertise on a regular basis. If they advertise regularly, the Federal Trade Commission probably hasn't kicked them out of business for poor service and the company is fairly stable.

Make sure the company offers a toll-free phone number (or any phone number for that matter). Any mail-order company that can't afford a toll-free number most likely can't afford to give much support to their customers, and doesn't want to field complaints.

Some mail-order companies offer overnight delivery if you use a credit card.

Call the dealer and find out how they handle credit card orders. The less reputable mail-order dealers bill your credit card before they ship your product, add various charges for credit card orders, or charge you a membership fee. If a dealer uses one of these tactics, shop elsewhere.

Because mail-order buying has the reputation for being risky, the better mail-order dealers offer 30-day money-back guarantees.

Buying Direct from the Publisher

Buying direct usually means paying the full retail price. Because buying direct has no advantage over buying through a dealer, you should only buy directly from a publisher if you cannot buy the program anywhere else or if the publisher offers a promotional deal. Many publishers sell $495 programs for $99 when they first introduce the program in order to get people talking about it.

Used Software

Buying used software can be the least expensive but also the most risky. When shopping for used software, make sure nothing is missing. Ideally, you want to buy a program that no one has opened yet. Check for the following items:

Registration Card. The registration card lists the legal owner of the program. If the previous owner has already mailed in the registration card, the company will send any newsletters or program upgrades to that person and not to you. Many companies let you transfer the registration to your name if you send in proof of purchase, such as the program disks or the first page of the manual. Every software publisher has a different procedure; call or write to the company to find out the exact procedures you need to follow.

209

Master Disks. Make sure all the master disks are included and check the directory to see if any of the program files have been modified. From the directory listing, you can see the dates of each file. If files have been modified, they may not work as described in the manuals.

User's Manual. Make sure you get the real manual, not a photocopy. Although manuals can be confusing to read and understand, they can be invaluable for finding what keys you need to press to enter commands. Because many programs come with several manuals (User, Reference, Getting Started), make sure you have them all; otherwise, you may not be able to use the program.

The Latest Version. Finally, make sure that you're buying the latest version of the program, or at least a version that you can live with. If you buy an old version, it may not offer all the features you expect.

> ▶ **Tip:** Although you generally want the latest program ver-
> sion, buying an older version can be a bargain if the program
> also contains the original registration card. If you buy an old pro-
> gram version and mail in the registration card, the publisher may
> offer the latest version for a small upgrade fee. Add the cost of the
> upgrade fee to the cost of the old program version, and the total
> cost might still be less than the cost for the latest program ver-
> sion.

Avoiding Problems

210

When you start shopping for software, watch out for yourself in order to
avoid some of the common pitfalls of first-time shoppers.

Because a single program may cost up to $495, many publishers
also offer 30-, 60-, or 90-day money-back guarantees to get you to try
the product.

Check the box that holds the program to determine the size of
disks included. Many software packages include both 5 1/4-inch and
3 1/2-inch disks, so you can use them in either type of disk drive. If the
package includes only one size, make sure it's the size you need. If the
program does not come with the right size floppy disks, you may be
able to send in a coupon to get the disks you need, but that means a
delay of several days.

Book Support

When you're shopping for software, consider the program's popularity.
If you choose a popular program, such as WordPerfect or Lotus 1-2-3,
you can be sure that you'll find several good books about the software
in your local bookstores. These books go beyond the documentation
that's included with the software by providing additional information,
such as:

▶ Step-by-step instructions that tell you how to use the program
to perform specific tasks

► Examples that give you hands-on practice using the program

► Tips, tricks, and hints for using the program more effectively

Company Reputation

The company that publishes a program can determine which program you decide to buy. Many software publishers have established excellent reputations through their dedicated service.

For example, WordPerfect pioneered the use of toll-free telephone support. Any time you need help using any program published by WordPerfect, call at their expense and WordPerfect's helpful technical staff answers your questions right away.

Borland International has also established a following with programs offering superior performance at a fair price. Their claim to fame is a 60-day money-back guarantee.

211

When you buy software from a large company such as Microsoft, Ashton-Tate, or Lotus Development, you're sure to receive excellent support and competent service.

> ► **Tip:** Don't forget shareware and public domain programs. The quality of shareware ranges from mediocre to superb. Many shareware programs began as commercial programs, but the company could not afford the high cost of advertising so they released them as shareware instead. Public domain programs are usually simple and require few instructions to use. Remember, you can legally copy, use, and give away public domain programs without paying for them. Because they are simple, however, you will rarely find a public domain word processor, spreadsheet, or database. (See Chapter 10.)

What You've Learned

Before you invest your savings in software, invest some time in research. Determine what you need and where to get it by keeping these points in mind:

► Use the program before you buy it and make sure it's exactly what you want.

► The first time you shop for software, buy the program from a reputable dealer.

► Make sure any program you buy comes with a money-back guarantee.

► Check out the software company's reputation before you send your check.

► If you plan on using your computer to perform a variety of general tasks, consider buying an integrated program.

► If you're looking for a bargain without risk, try shareware programs.

Chapter 14

Maintaining and Securing Your Computer

In This Chapter

▶ *What you can do to make sure your computer lives long past its warranty*

▶ *Protecting your monitor from permanent damage*

▶ *Protecting your computer against power surges*

▶ *Protecting the information stored on your floppy disks*

▶ *Protecting your files from accidental or deliberate modifications*

▶ *Encrypting your files to protect your secrets*

▶ *Protecting your computer against viruses*

▶ *How hackers can take over your computer*

When you finally get a computer and bring it home, you need to start thinking about what you must do to take care of it. By following a few simple rules and performing some basic maintenance activities on a regular basis, you can ensure that your computer lives a long and healthy life.

In addition to caring for your computer, you must protect it from outsiders. More importantly, you must protect the information that's stored in your computer. The world of computers attracts a wide range of practical jokers who are determined to destroy your information. This chapter helps you defend against these invasions.

Maintaining Your Computer

Maintaining a computer takes very little time and effort; yet few people perform the steps necessary to keep their computers in good condition. If you want a reliable computer, you need to spend time taking care of it.

Finding a Place for Your Computer

Put your computer in a cool, dry place out of direct sunlight. If it gets too hot around your computer, it may overheat, burning out some of its circuits and costing you money.

Make sure the place you choose is fairly clean and dust free. For example, don't set up your computer next to the clothes dryer, where lint can pour through every opening.

To provide more desk space, many people turn their computers on the side and tuck them under their desk. This is fine—it won't do any damage to your computer. However, if your computer has a hard disk, format your hard disk after you've turned the computer on its side. While not always necessary, this precaution can prevent hard disk failures in the future.

> ▶ **Tip:** Remember, once your computer is set up, turn it on and leave the system on (except the monitor) for a couple of days for burn-in to make sure that your computer will outlast its warranty. You can use your computer during this time—just don't turn it off when you're done. If the computer fails, return it before the warranty runs out. Many computer manufacturers put their computers through burn-in periods before shipping, and many dealers do so as well. Nevertheless, you should do your own burn-in after you get the computer home.

Protecting the Monitor

You turn your monitor off for the burn-in because it can suffer damage if left on for extended periods.The image on the screen can physically

214

etch itself into the screen, leaving a permanent ghost. The only way to remove these ghost images is to buy a new CRT (the picture tube of your monitor).

To protect your monitor from ghost images, turn down the brightness of your monitor when you're not using it. You can also get a screen saver program that automatically turns off your monitor for you. If you don't press a key for several minutes, the program assumes you've walked away and shuts off the monitor. Press a key, and the monitor's back on.

Protecting Against Power Drops and Surges

Because computers depend on a steady and reliable source of electricity, don't plug your computer into the same circuits with other major appliances, such as washing machines, refrigerators, and air conditioners. Each time one of these power drainers kicks in, it'll steal power away from your computer, possibly destroying whatever information is stored in the computer's RAM.

215

Depending on where you live, power drops may be fairly common and out of your control, even if you plug your computer into a circuit by itself. To solve these problems, many people buy *surge suppressors* or *uninterrupted power supplies* (*UPS*) to regulate their electricity (see Figure 14-1).

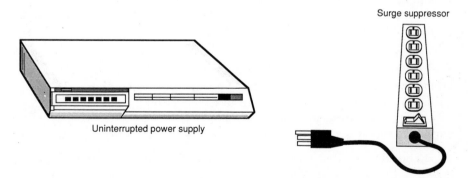

Figure 14-1. Surge suppressor and uninterrupted power supply.

Surge suppressors protect your computer against sudden power increases that can damage components inside your computer. The surge suppressor protects your hardware but it will not protect against power drops that may destroy information.

To protect your computer against power outages or drops, you need to use an uninterrupted power supply. A UPS is nothing more than a battery. The moment the power stops, the UPS turns on its own power to keep your computer running, giving you at least enough time to save your work to disk before the power outage wipes out your RAM. A better UPS may even let you continue working for up to 10 hours during a power outage.

Keeping Your Computer Clean

216

Do not smoke, eat, or drink around your computer. Smoke particles can settle on the surfaces of floppy disks making the disks unreadable. If the smoke gets inside your computer it could cover the sensitive disk drive heads, making it difficult or impossible for the drive to read your disks.

Likewise, don't eat or drink around a computer; food particles and liquids can fall between the cracks in a keyboard, causing short-circuits and interfering with the operation of the keys. True to its namesake, a mouse will pick up every crumb on your table. The mechanical one gets gummed up in no time.

If you absolutely must drink around a computer, find a place where you can store your drink below the level of the keyboard and computer. That way if you spill your drink, the liquid falls on the floor (or on your shoes) instead of in the keyboard, monitor, or computer.

Dust your computer once in a while with a clean, dry cloth—don't spray anything on the computer. Put dust covers over your keyboard and monitor when you are not using them. To keep your keyboard dust-free, buy a can of compressed air from a photography shop, and spray the dust out from between your keys; just make sure that you spray the dust away from the rest of your computer.

The biggest dust collector of your entire system is the monitor. Again, when you wipe the monitor, use a clean, dry cloth. Anything wet can seep into the monitor and damage the circuits.

Manufacturers suggest you clean your computer's disk drives every two weeks, although some users have used their computers for years and never done so. If you do decide to play it safe and clean your disk drive heads, you can use a special cleaning kit. It requires that you spray a fluid on a special floppy disk and insert this disk into a disk drive. As this special disk spins around, the cleaning fluid wipes the disk drive heads clean.

If you want, you can perform the same process manually by soaking a cotton swab in alcohol and rubbing the disk drive heads yourself, as shown in Figure 14-2. This cleaning process rubs any magnetic disk residue off the disk drive heads.

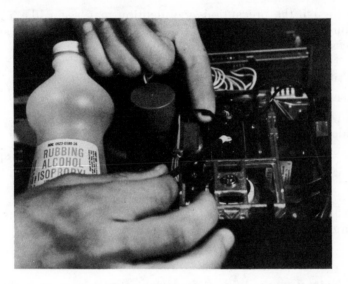

Figure 14-2. Cleaning the disk drive heads. *(Reprinted, by permission, from Brenner Microcomputing, Inc.,* IBM PC Advanced Troubleshooting & Repair.)

217

Caring for Floppy Disks

Keep floppy disks away from magnetic fields because they could erase or damage your files.

Common sources of magnetic fields include telephones, stereos, and televisions. If you're traveling with floppy disks, don't put the disks through any metal detectors or X-ray machines—have the security guards inspect the disks separately.

Securing Your Computer Equipment

When you've found a comfortable home for your computer and taken all the necessary precautions to protect it from the natural elements, start thinking about protecting it from outsiders. This means protecting both your hardware and your data from theft and intrusion.

Although the precautions we mention may seem like a hassle at first, you'll find that developing the proper work habits and performing the necessary precautions save you time in the long run:

► Write down the serial number in case of theft.
► Keep the computer in a locked room.
► If you have several computers in your place of business, consider installing burglar alarms.
► Ask your computer dealer about protective cases or special locks that clamp the computer to a table or desk.

218

If your computer has a hard disk, protecting the computer in this way also ensures that precious data stored on the hard disk is not lost in a burglary.

> ► **Note:** The single most important step you must perform in secure the information in your system is to make backup copies of your files—often! Many users make backup copies and store them in a disk file right next to their computers. It's convenient, but it's also dumb. Burglars rarely practice the courtesy of leaving backups, and fires are even less thoughtful. If you use a computer at work, take the backup disks home with you at the end of the day. If you work at home, store the disks in a separate room. It's not very convenient, but it's a lot safer.

Using Passwords

If you need to prevent other people from using your data, look for programs that offer a password feature. Only people who know the password can access certain directories or files.

When using passwords, avoid one-letter ones and common passwords like "Open," "Love," and "Password." The most effective passwords are those that contain a mix of letters and numbers. For example, combine your initials with your phone number to come up with something like W6E9W1. One last note—don't forget your password!

If you want even more protection, purchase a special security program for your entire computer. With these programs, anyone can turn on your computer, but they can't use it until they enter the correct password.

Many computers even come with a lock and key that let you physically lock your keyboard and hard disk. Without the key, no one can even start up the computer.

Encrypting Files

219

Encrypting a file essentially scrambles the file on disk; it's like shredding paper. When you want to read a file, enter the required password and the program automatically pieces the file back together.

To encrypt a file, you need to use special file encrypting programs such as the one that comes with PC Tools Deluxe. For added security, you can encrypt a file two or more times, using different passwords. Even if someone knows your passwords, they must enter them in the correct order.

Protecting Against Trojan Horse and Virus Programs

You already encountered Trojan horse and virus programs in Chapter 10. Although such programs cannot physically damage any parts of your computer, they can destroy every file on your hard disk. Because that could represent months or years of work, it's worth knowing a little bit about preventing them.

To protect your computer and files against Trojan horse programs, don't let anyone copy or run programs on your computer without your permission. You don't have to worry so much about commercial programs (such as Microsoft Word or Lotus 1-2-3)—these programs are safe. The programs you do need to worry about are those copied from an electronic bulletin board or copies of programs from an unreliable source.

When in doubt, test the program on another computer that does not have a hard disk or that has unimportant files. That way, if the program is a Trojan horse, you haven't destroyed valuable data.

Unlike Trojan horse programs, that are actually independent programs, a virus hides itself in a host program, making it more difficult to prevent infection. And since computers are so good at trading information, they are also very good at spreading these viruses. Take the following precautions:

Isolate Your System. Don't let anyone insert a floppy disk in your computer without your knowledge. Any disk could contain a virus. If you're hooked up to a modem, this type of prevention is not very effective.

Write-Protect. A virus infects only program files, not data files, such as those you create. Write-protect any program disks that you purchase (see Chapter 4). You can still run the programs as usual, but no virus can write itself onto any of your program files.

Eliminate Program Files from Data Disks. For Macintosh computers, virus programs infect the hidden Desktop file that exists on every Macintosh-formatted floppy disk. Since you cannot erase the Desktop file, this form of prevention won't work. For IBM and compatible computers, virus programs commonly infect files ending with the .EXE or .COM file extension. Erasing .EXE and .COM files from your data disks will prevent infection.

Change File Attribute to Read Only. On an IBM, viruses tend to infect a file called COMMAND.COM. Formatting a disk with the FORMAT /S command automatically puts the COMMAND.COM file on a disk. To prevent a virus from infecting the COMMAND.COM file, use the ATTRIB command to change the file attribute to read only. This is essentially the same principle as write-protecting a disk—you can read the file and use it, but you can't write anything on it, including a virus. To change a file attribute to read only, type the following ATTRIB command: **ATTRIB +R command.com**

220

> ► **Note:** Normally the COMMAND.COM file is never modified once it is created. If the file size looks unusually large or the date of your COMMAND.COM file looks too recent, a virus may be infecting the file.

Using Anti-Virus Programs

Some virus programs can still infect a file, even if you have changed the file attribute to read only. To protect your data from these types of viruses, you need an anti-virus program, which keeps tabs on the file size and date of your files. If either changes suddenly, the program beeps a warning to let you know that a virus is trying to attack your computer. Other anti-virus programs work by infecting your files before a real virus program can infect them. Because your files are already infected by the anti-virus program, no other virus programs can infect your files, making your computer safe.

Some popular anti-virus programs for the IBM include FluShot+ and the Panda Utilities. If you have a Macintosh, popular anti-virus programs include SAM and Virex.

Hacker Prevention   221

The term *hackers* loosely refers to a person so enthralled with computers that food, drink, and sleep are sacrificed in favor of more time playing with the computer. Hackers can dial into another computer, take control, and destroy data, but only if your computer meets these criteria:

▶ It has a modem.
▶ Both the computer and the modem are left on.
▶ It is running a program that answers the phone when another computer calls.

To prevent a hacker from gaining control of your computer, just turn your computer or modem off when you're not using it. If you need to leave your computer and modem on to wait for a call, don't rely on passwords to keep hackers from away. Instead, get a *call-back device*, which answers the phone, requests a password, then hangs up the phone and then calls a number for that particular password.

What You've Learned

If you've gone shopping for a computer, you know how expensive they are, so protect your equipment. When you get the computer home, take the necessary precautions to secure it, and keep the following points in mind:

▶ Find a place for your computer that is cool and dry and free from dust and smoke.

▶ When you first get your computer home, leave it on (except the monitor) for at least two days straight to test its circuits.

▶ If you're going to leave your monitor on for more than a half hour without working on it, turn the brightness down.

▶ A surge suppressor protects against power surges. An uninterrupted power supply protects against power drops or outages that may cause you to lose data.

▶ Magnetic fields can erase or damage files stored on floppy disks.

▶ The best way to protect the data stored on disks is to make backup copies of your files and store them in a safe place.

▶ Passwords provide a limited form of protection for your data and computer.

▶ File encryption physically scrambles your data so no one can use it.

▶ For additional security, you can encrypt the same file several times using different passwords.

▶ The best protection against a Trojan horse program is to test the program on a computer without a hard disk before using the program.

▶ Virus programs live in existing program files, so write-protect your program disks and change program file attributes to read only.

▶ Special anti-virus programs are available that help prevent viruses and diagnose infections.

▶ Hackers are people who know how to break into another computer through the telephone lines.

Chapter 15

Where To Go from Here

In This Chapter

▶ *Where to look for more information about computers and software*

▶ *Sharing information at users groups*

▶ *What to expect from training courses*

▶ *Keeping your equipment up to date*

▶ *Deciding whether to upgrade your old computer or buy a new one*

▶ *Expanding the capabilities of your computer*

The computer industry has become one of the world's many informal colleges. Sure, you can take computer classes in universities, but the real excitement is happening outside the schools. Small computer companies spring up overnight with new, improved equipment and programs, and word hits the streets soon after. If the product gets thumbs up from a large group of users, everyone learns the program, sharing techniques and tricks.

In order to keep up on late-breaking developments in the computer industry, stay in touch with some of the sources that provide this information.

Books

Private publishers develop three categories of books that provide comprehensive instructions on all phases of computer use:

▶ How-to books

▶ Books of tips, tricks, and hints

▶ Books with example applications

How-to books provide step-by-step instructions in more detail than the manuals that come with programs, and include examples that tell you exactly what keys to press and what commands you need to enter.

224

Most how-to books give a brief overview of the operating system and tell you the basics you need to know before starting. If you already know how to use a program, these books provide a quick reference for some of the features you use less often.

Tips, tricks, and hints books provide information on using a program more effectively. You learn how to use undocumented or poorly documented features of a program and more efficient ways to perform a task—secrets about features that the software publisher didn't know.

If you want to see a program in action, get an example application book. These books provide tutorials that lead you through the program with detailed examples. In other words, you learn by doing. These books are excellent if you want to learn how to use a program before starting on your own work. If you want to use the book to perform specific tasks, you can modify the book examples to meet your particular needs.

Magazines

Although books provide more detailed information about a program, magazines provide more recent information. In addition to advertisements and software reviews that tell you what's new and what's good, magazines also provide tips, tricks, and hints for using a particular program, how to use it for a specific application, and tutorials for using a program's little known features.

Because magazines cater to particular user groups, find a magazine that contains the information you need the most. Magazines can be divided into four groups:

► Business
► Technical
► General
► Specialized

Business magazines, such as *PC World* and *MacWorld*, focus on using programs for solving common business problems. They provide helpful hints for printing mailing labels, managing payroll, and using the computer in production. Advertisements, software reviews, and articles that appear in these magazines emphasize convenience, ease of use, and value. If you're using the computer to automate your business, the tips included are well worth the subscription price.

225

Technical magazines, such as *PC Magazine* and *MacUser*, focus on program features: for instance, speed, capacity, and compatibility. These magazines assume that the reader knows computer basics and appreciates the importance of particular features. If you want to understand why one computer or program may be better than another, or if you plan on servicing your own computer or writing your own programs, consider subscribing to a technical magazine.

General magazines, such as *Home Office Computing*, focus on using a computer for home or work. These magazines assume that you're a beginner, so they often publish articles explaining common topics, such as how to use a spreadsheet or how to choose the right computer for your needs.

Specialized magazines are directed at narrow user groups such as database programmers, doctors, lawyers, and accountants. They include such titles as *Data Based Advisor* (about databases), *Computer Language* (about different programming techniques), and *M.D. Computing* (for doctors who use computers in their work). Because the information published in the magazine relates to such a narrow field, you can find extremely detailed information and plenty of helpful hints.

Classes

If all the books and manuals you first encounter seem like too much at one time, consider taking a class on the program you want to use. You can learn how to use a program much faster than you could on your own, and if you get in a jam, the instructor can help.

If you have the money, try to take the class at a private school or business college. Although public schools and colleges may have excellent instructors, they often don't have the funds to buy up-to-date equipment. You may get stuck learning a program on an obsolete computer.

To establish credibility, private schools may hire instructors trained directly by software publishers. For example, the WordPerfect Corporation offers special training classes given by a company representative. After you pass the class you can claim that you're WordPerfect certified.

User Groups

User groups consist of people who meet regularly to share ideas and information, to buy and sell equipment, and to learn more about a particular computer or program. Most user groups are centered around a specific computer or program.

As part of their meetings, many user groups invite company representatives to demonstrate their latest products and to answer questions. These meetings are great for keeping up on the latest features of a program. In addition, many users groups offer their own classes, for free or for a modest price, to help users learn about their systems.

Newsletters

Many independent publishers print newsletters containing tips, tricks, and hints for using specific programs such as dBASE III Plus or Lotus

1-2-3. Although expensive (subscriptions can cost up to several hundred dollars a year for a monthly newsletter), these newsletters come packed with useful information that can actually save you money and make you more productive.

Consultants

You can hire a consultant as a private tutor to show you how to use your computer or as an expert to help you automate your business. In either case, the consultant can be very valuable.

The problem with consultants is that the less reliable ones make you depend on their services; that is, they won't teach you anything. Whenever you run into a problem, the consultant shows up, fixes the problem and takes your money, even when you could have fixed the problem yourself.

227

The best way to defend yourself against getting taken is to learn as much about the system as possible. Ask the consultant a lot of questions. If you're having trouble getting the information you need to become independent, consider hiring someone else.

Videotapes

The latest craze in the world of training is instructional videos. These videos let you watch someone using the computer or program to perform common tasks. By watching the video and following along with the user manual, you get the guided instruction of a classroom instructor with the convenience of a book.

Keeping Your Equipment Up to Date

Even if you purchase the most modern computer, some day you'll find that you can't run the newest program or the computer can't hold the information you need to store. When this happens, you are faced with a choice: buy a new computer or upgrade the old one?

Replace or Upgrade?

If you need to improve a single feature of your computer, replacing the entire computer is unnecessary. For example, if you need a color monitor or a hard disk drive, you can usually buy these items separately and install them yourself or have a technician install them.

If you bought your computer several years ago and find that you need to upgrade several of its features in order to use it effectively, buying a new computer can save you money and frustration. When a company builds a computer, they design it to work with all the equipment available at the time. If you try to upgrade several features of a computer, you may run into problems later.

228

> ▶ **Tip:** Remember, although computer manufacturers design and build computers to handle the most recent programs, they leave room for growth. The computer may have a couple extra ports and several open expansion slots that let you plug in additional, more advanced equipment (see Chapter 12).

Before you start fiddling with the insides of your computer, get a book on the subject. Upgrade and repair books give helpful instructions for troubleshooting problems, taking apart the computer, and performing the required steps. These books also contain safety precautions to prevent you from harming yourself or your computer.

Expanding Random Access Memory

To add more RAM to your computer, you have two choices. You can plug the memory chips directly into the motherboard or you can plug them into a memory expansion board, and then plug this board into the open expansion slot.

You can also upgrade by adding any or all of the following:

▶ A new monitor
▶ A new disk drive
▶ Ports
▶ An internal modem
▶ An internal clock
▶ Accelerator boards
▶ Multifunction boards

If you want to add a new monitor to your computer, you also need to add a new video board, which plugs into your computer's expansion slot. The monitor plugs into the video board.

A complete disk drive kit includes a disk drive controller board, the disk drive, and a cable connecting the two. To add a disk drive to your computer, plug the disk drive controller board into an expansion slot and the disk drive into an open drive bay.

229

To add a port to your computer, just plug the expansion board for the port you need into the expansion slot.

An internal modem is a single expansion board. Plug the modem into an expansion slot and then plug a phone line into the back of the modem.

Newer computers have built-in clocks with batteries that keep track of time even after you turn off your computer. Older computers may not have this feature. To determine if your computer has a built-in clock, type `date` or `time` at the DOS prompt. If your computer displays a date like `1-1-80` or a time like `0:00:01`, then you know that your computer does not have a built-in clock. Add a clock in either of two ways. Some companies sell a clock unit. You plug it directly into your computer's processor socket and plug the processor on top of the clock. The other way is to install the clock into an expansion slot.

To make your computer run faster, you can plug an accelerator board into your computer's expansion slot. An accelerator board contains a faster processor and a cable. To install it, plug the accelerator board into an open expansion slot, remove your old processor, and plug the accelerator board cable into the old processor socket.

An accelerator board makes your computer run faster, but not as fast as a new computer that uses the same processor. If you want the speed of a new computer, you need to replace the entire motherboard. It's expensive, but not nearly as expensive as a new computer.

A computer only contains a limited number of expansion slots, and you don't want to plug up every expansion slot with a different expansion board. To conserve expansion slots, many companies sell multifunction boards that combine many features on a single board:

▶ Expanded memory

▶ A serial port

▶ A parallel port

▶ A game port

▶ A clock

What You've Learned

230

Once you learn the basics of your computer and one or two programs, don't stop there. Get involved in user groups, buy a subscription to one of the general magazines, and keep reading books on whatever subject interests you. After a few months, you'll emerge with a clearer understanding of computers and of how they can help you do your work. Remember these tips:

▶ Books from independent publishers help you learn a program quickly and use the program effectively.

▶ Magazines provide more up-to-date information about the latest equipment and programs.

▶ Classes provide a quick way to learn a program and may offer certification.

▶ User groups can give you the information you need to get started and to keep track of the latest developments.

▶ Although consultants can help you get your system up and running, make sure you learn how to operate the system for yourself.

▶ Even the most powerful computer becomes obsolete eventually.

▶ To keep up with the advances in technology, you can upgrade your computer by plugging expansion boards into the open slots on the motherboard.

▶ Accelerator boards make your computer run faster.

▶ Multifunction boards combine several advanced features on a single board.

Appendix A

Glossary of Computer Terms

8086 The microprocessor used in many IBM PC/XT compatible computers.

8087 The math coprocessor that works with the 8088 or 8086 microprocessor.

8088 The microprocessor used in IBM PC/XT computers.

68000 The microprocessor used in the Macintosh Plus, Macintosh SE.

68020 The microprocessor used in the Macintosh II computer.

68881 The math coprocessor that works with the 68000 and 68020 microprocessors.

68030 The microprocessor used in the Macintosh IIci/IIcx/IIc and the Macintosh SE/30.

80286 The microprocessor used in IBM AT and compatible computers. Used in computers that include "286" in the name, such as the Compaq 286 or the AST Premium 286.

80287 The math coprocessor that works with the 80286 microprocessor.

80386 The microprocessor used in computers that include "386" in the name, such as Compaq 386 or AST Premium 386. Faster than the 80286 microprocessor.

80387 The math coprocessor that works with the 80386 microprocessor.

80486 The microprocessor used in computers that include "486" in the name, such as Compaq 486 or AST Premium 486. Faster than the 80386 microprocessor.

Accelerator board An expansion board that plugs in a computer to make the computer work faster.

Access time The amount of time a hard disk drive needs to find data. Often measured in milliseconds, abbreviated as ms, such as "28ms."

Active directory The directory that the computer performs commands on unless instructed otherwise.

Active drive The disk drive that the computer performs commands on unless instructed otherwise.

Active window The displayed window that the computer performs commands on.

Ada Programming language designed by the Department of Defense. Similar to Pascal. See also Modula-2 and Pascal.

232

Algorithm A set of steps, like a cookbook recipe, that leads to a specific result. When writing programs, algorithms define how the program works.

Application A program that performs a specific task, such as a word processor, spreadsheet, or database. Part of an application package.

Application package The complete collection of program, manuals, and reference cards or templates.

Application software A redundant term used by people to sound impressive when talking about computers, much like telling someone that you own a "car automobile."

ASCII Acronym for American Standard Code for Information Interchange.

ASCII file A file containing characters that can be used by any program on any computer. Sometimes called a text file or an ASCII text file.

Assembler A program that translates assembly language programs into machine code. Used by programmers for writing programs.

Assembly language A language for programming a specific microprocessor, such as the 8088 or the 68000. Used for writing fast and small programs.

Auto-dialer A feature that lets a modem and communications software dial phone calls automatically.

AUTOEXEC.BAT An optional batch file that performs DOS commands on IBM and compatible computers.

Automatic hyphenation A feature that hyphenates words automatically. Often found in word processors and desktop publishing programs.

Automatic pagination A feature that automatically breaks text into pages. Often found in word processors and desktop publishing programs.

Auto-redial A feature that lets a modem and communications software repeatedly dial a phone number until it connects.

Backup disk A duplicate copy of a floppy disk that preserves your files in case you ruin them.

Backup file A duplicate copy of a file that preserves your work in case you should ruin the original file.

.BAK Common file extension for backup files.

BASIC Acronym for Beginner's All-Purpose Symbolic Instruction Code. An easy-to-learn programming language available for nearly all personal computers.

.BAT File extension for DOS batch files.

Batch file An ASCII text file containing DOS commands. See also ASCII file.

Baud A unit for measuring the speed of data transmission, usually used to describe the speeds of modems, such as 2,400 baud.

Baud rate The speed at which data transfers between two items, such as between two computers connected through modems.

BIOS Acronym for Basic Input/Output System. Every computer has a BIOS chip, sometimes called the ROM BIOS chip.

BIOS chip A special chip that contains instructions the computer needs to start working. With IBM compatible computers, the type of BIOS chip used determines the hardware and software compatibility of the computer with a genuine IBM computer.

Bomb A destructive program set to "explode" at a certain time or under a certain condition, such as on April 1 or when a database no longer contains a certain employee's name. When a bomb "explodes," it may erase important data. See also Trojan horse and virus.

Boot Describes turning on a computer as in "boot up" the computer. Originates from the phrase, "pulling yourself up by the bootstraps."

Buffer A space in the computer's memory for temporarily storing data. A print buffer stores data in memory until the printer is ready.

Bug An error in a program that prevents the program from running correctly. Originates when a moth short-circuited a connection in one of the first computers, preventing the computer from working.

Bulletin Board System (BBS) A computer that can receive phone calls so that callers may send or receive files or messages for others. Typical uses for a BBS include uploading and downloading programs, sending and receiving electronic mail, and playing games with the computer or with other callers.

233

Bundled software Programs that come for free with a computer.

Burn-in A period of time, usually 48 hours, when the computer is on constantly to test its circuits. Dealers put computers through burn-in periods to make sure the computers work. The theory is that if you can leave a computer on for 48 hours, its circuits are reliable.

Bus A series of wire connections that carry electronic information through a computer.

C Popular programming language originally used for developing the UNIX operating system. Currently used for writing programs of all types.

Cache Part of memory that makes your computer run faster by holding the most recently accessed data from a disk. The next time the computer needs the data, it accesses it from memory rather than from the disk, which would be slower. Sometimes called a RAM cache.

Cache size The amount of memory allocated for the cache, measured in kilobytes (K) such as 64K.

234

Cancel To stop or prevent a command from running. Most often chosen by pressing the Esc key.

Case-sensitive The ability to distinguish between upper- and lowercase letters. Often used when searching for words in a word processor or database.

Cell The part of a spreadsheet that contains a number, label, or formula.

Characters per inch (CPI) Unit of measurement for the number of characters that will print in one horizontal inch. Sometimes called pitch.

Characters per second (cps) Unit of measurement for the speed of data transfer. Most often used to describe printing speed, such as 132 cps.

Character style The stylistic appearance of text, such as italics, bold, or underline. Also called typestyle.

Check box A small box associated with an option in a dialog box. A check mark in the check box means the option is on. An empty check box means the option is off. More than one check box can be checked. See also Dialog box and Radio button.

Class A One of two FCC classifications for electronic equipment. Class A means that the item can be used in an office setting.

Class B One of two FCC classifications for electronic equipment. Class B means that the item can be used in the home or office setting. Class B is a more stringent requirement than class A.

Click To move the mouse pointer over an object or icon and press and release the mouse button once.

Clipboard Temporary storage that holds text and graphics. The cut and copy commands put text or graphics into the clipboard, erasing the clipboard's previous contents. The paste command copies clipboard data to a document. When you turn off the computer, the contents of the clipboard disappear.

Clock speed The speed at which a microprocessor performs calculations, often measured in megahertz (MHz). Common clock speeds range from 4.77 MHz to 33 MHz.

Clone Term used to describe a computer made by a local computer dealer that uses the same parts and programs as a more popular computer. Also used to describe a program that mimics a more popular program. Often a derogatory term.

Close The act of removing a window from the screen or removing an open file.

Close box The small box that appears in the upper-left corner of a window. Clicking in this close box with the mouse removes the window from the screen.

Code A set of instructions written in a programming language. Also called source code.

235

Color Graphics Adapter (CGA) A color graphics standard that defines the resolution of a program. CGA video boards and monitors display text with noticeable graininess. The resolution of CGA graphics is 640 × 200. Newer computers use EGA or VGA graphics. See Enhanced Graphics Adapter and Virtual Graphics Array.

Column A vertical section of printed text on a page, or a vertical row of cells in a spreadsheet.

Compatible Term used to describe a computer that uses the same parts and programs as a more popular computer such as IBM or Macintosh. Compatible computers, such as Epson or Compaq, have national recognition.

Compile The process of translating a programming language, such as BASIC or Pascal, into machine code. See also Assemble.

Compiler A program that translates a program, written in a language such as BASIC or Pascal, into machine code. See also Assembler.

Configuration The combination of hardware and software making a complete computer system.

Configure To specify how the hardware and software are connected together.

Context-sensitive Ability to perceive the current conditions of an event. Often used to describe help systems as context-sensitive help systems.

Continuous-form Paper, mailing labels, or cards, designed for computer printers and connected through perforations at defined lengths.

Coprocessor A microprocessor that works with a computer's existing microprocessor. Often used to describe a math coprocessor, which is a special microprocessor specifically for calculating math.

Copy protection A method that makes copying a floppy disk theoretically impossible. Most often found on games to prevent people from illegally duplicating and distributing the disks to others.

CPU Acronym for Central Processing Unit. See also Microprocessor.

Crash What happens when the computer stops working unexpectedly.

Current directory The directory that the computer will use when given commands.

Current drive The disk drive that the computer uses when given commands.

Cut Removing text or graphics from a document and placing it in the Clipboard. See also Clipboard.

236

Cyclic Redundancy Check (CRC) An error-checking method used when transmitting data. Often used when sending and receiving data using modems and communications programs.

Cylinder A pair of tracks that lie opposite one another on both sides of a hard disk platter.

Daisywheel printer A printer that uses a wheel made up of "petals" that each contain one character. Printing occurs by spinning the wheel and striking individual petals.

Data Information stored in the computer as numbers, letters, and special symbols such as punctuation marks.

Database A collection of organized information stored in a disk file. Also refers to a program that creates, organizes, and sorts information. Examples of a database include dBASE IV, Paradox, and R:Base.

Data conversion The process of changing data stored in a particular way to another way.

dBASE Popular database program, by Ashton-Tate, that runs on the IBM computer family. Versions include dBASE II, dBASE III, dBASE III Plus, and dBASE IV.

.DBF File extension used for files created using the dBase program.

Debug The process of locating an error or bug in a program.

Debugger A special program designed to simplify the process of locating errors or bugs in a program.

Dedicated file server A computer used exclusively for running a network.

Default A predefined action or command that the computer chooses unless you specify otherwise.

Desktop The computer screen displaying a menu bar, windows, and icons. Commonly used to describe the Macintosh and Microsoft Windows.

Desktop presentation Presenting text, video, and graphics on the computer for display to others.

Desktop publishing (DTP) Using a computer to design and print pages for publication.

Desktop video Using a computer to create and edit video images.

Dialog Communication between a person and a computer.

Dialog box A box containing a message and one or more options for the user to choose.

Digitize Convert an image into a series of dots. Often used to store images on disk for the computer.

DIP switch A set of small on/off switches mounted on circuit boards used for choosing different options for the circuit board.

Directory A list of files stored on a disk. Directories within existing directories are called subdirectories.

237

Disk A round, flat, magnetic storage medium. Floppy disks are made of flexible material and enclosed in 5 1/4-inch or 3 1/2-inch protective cases. Hard disks are rigid.

Disk drive A device that reads and writes data to a floppy or hard disk.

Disk drive head The part of a disk drive that reads data from a floppy or hard disk.

Diskless workstation A computer on a network that has no disk drives. Used primarily for accessing files through the network.

Disk Operating System (DOS) A program that tells the computer how to work. MS-DOS is the common disk operating system for IBM and compatible computers.

Display A screen or monitor that presents information.

Document Data created by a program. Most commonly used to describe a word processor file. See also File.

Documentation The printed instruction manuals that are supposed to explain how to use equipment or programs.

Dot matrix print Printed type that uses a series of dots for printing characters.

Dot matrix printer A printer that uses 9-pins, 18-pins, or 24-pins for printing. The higher the number of pins, the sharper the printing looks.

Dots per inch (dpi) A unit of measurement for the resolution of monitors, laser printers, and scanners. Laser printers tend to offer 300 dpi (90,000 dots per square inch).

Double-click Clicking the mouse button twice in rapid succession. Double-clicking usually selects and opens a file.

Download To copy files from another computer (usually a mainframe or electronic bulletin board) through a modem.

Downloadable fonts Typefaces stored on disk that must be copied into the printer's memory before you can use that particular font.

Draft quality High-speed but low-resolution printing commonly found with dot matrix printers.

Drag To move the mouse pointer on an object, hold down the mouse button, and move the mouse while keeping the mouse button held down. Often used to select groups of items or to move pictures around the screen.

DRAM Acronym for Dynamic Random Access Memory. See also Dynamic RAM.

238

Drive head The part of a disk drive that moves across a floppy or hard disk surface, reading and writing data on it.

Driver A program that lets the computer send or receive information from an external device, such as a printer or a mouse.

DTP Acronym for DeskTop Publishing.

Dvorak keyboard An alternate keyboard layout designed to be faster and easier to learn for typing.

Dynamic RAM Type of memory chip that requires recharging periodically to avoid losing data. Less expensive but slower memory chip than static RAM or SRAM chips.

Edit To change text or graphics.

Editor A program that uses ASCII characters and saves files in ASCII format. Cannot change fonts, formats, or styles. Commonly used for writing programs. Also called a text editor.

EDLIN Acronym for EDit LINe. A simple editor that comes with MS-DOS and lets you edit one line at a time.

EISA Acronym for Extended Industry Standard Architecture, which is an agreed-upon standard for building the bus in an IBM compatible computer.

E-mail Acronym for Electronic mail, which lets people send and receive messages stored solely on the computer.

EMS Acronym for Expanded Memory Specification, which is a special way for IBM computers to use more memory beyond 640K. Developed jointly by Lotus, Intel, and Microsoft and sometimes called the LIM specification.

Emulate To imitate the way another item works. Often used to describe the ability of one printer to act like another, such as "Epson printer emulation."

Encapsulated PostScript (EPS) A special file format, containing text and graphics, created using the PostScript programming language.

Enhanced graphics adapter (EGA) A color graphics standard that defines the resolution of a program. EGA video boards and monitors display text with 640 × 350 resolution. Officially abandoned as a graphics standard in favor of VGA graphics. See also Virtual Graphics Array.

Enhanced small device interface (ESDI) An interface that speeds up disk drive access.

Erasable disk An erasable optical disk capable of storing up to 2.6 gigabytes of information.

Error checking The ability to check errors during data transfer, most commonly while using a modem and communications software.

.EXE An executable program file for IBM and compatible computers. Program files typically have an acronym that resembles the program name, such as WP.EXE for WordPerfect and 123.EXE for Lotus 1-2-3.

239

Execute To run a program or command.

Federal Communications Commission (FCC) A government agency that sets standards and regulates communications in the United States.

Field In a database record, a field is a specified area for specific types of data. Examples might be a name field, a telephone field, or a ZIP code field.

File A collection of information stored on a floppy or hard disk. Files always have a file name to identify them.

File Allocation Table (FAT) A record, on a floppy or hard disk, that keeps track of each file's location on the disk.

File extension A period followed by up to three characters, usually used to identify the file type for IBM computers.

File locking A method to prevent two or more users from modifying the same file.

File name A name to identify files on a floppy or hard disk. With IBM computers, file names can be up to 8 characters long. File names can be up to 31 characters long with Macintosh computers.

File server A computer and program that controls a local area network (LAN).

Fixed disk Another name for a hard disk drive.

Floppy disk A disk made of flexible plastic, coated with a magnetic surface to store data. Floppy disks come in 5 1/4-inch and 3 1/2-inch sizes.

Font A set of letters, numbers, and symbols that appear in a particular typeface, size, and style.

Footprint The amount of space a desktop computer uses.

Form feed To advance a page to a specified position in a printer.

Format To design pages using such word processing options as margins, running heads, centered text, graphics, etc.

Friction feed A setting that lets a printer advance paper between the platen by friction. See also tractor feed.

Gas plasma screen A highly legible orange screen often used in laptop and portable computers.

Gigabyte (Gb) A unit of measurement for one billion bytes.

Graphical user interface (GUI) A program that makes a computer easier to use by letting the user point to pictures representing files.

Graphics A symbol, such as a line, oval, rectangle, or circle.

240

Hacker Slang term for someone who is particularly skilled and knowledgeable about computers. Often used to describe people who can perform unusual tricks with a computer, such as breaking into other computers.

Hard copy Pages containing data that a printer produced. Also called a printout.

Hard disk A metal disk able to store more information than a floppy disk. Hard disks are usually installed internally or externally.

Head The device that reads or writes data to a floppy or hard disk.

Hypertext A way of linking text to other text or pictures.

Icon A graphic image that represents another object, such as a file on a disk.

Import To load a file created by another program.

Index To rearrange a list of information without physically moving data to different locations. Often used with databases.

Initialize To reset a computer or program to some starting values. When used to describe floppy or hard disks, the term means the same as format. See Format.

Input To feed information into a computer through a device such as the keyboard.

Integrated package A program that combines the features of several programs, such as a word processor, spreadsheet, database, and communications program. Also called integrated program.

Interface A link between two objects, such as a computer and a person. Such a link is often called a user interface, which refers to the way a person gives commands to the computer.

Interleave The relationship between the rate at which a hard disk spins and the way it organizes files on the disk. Don't worry about it.

Internal drive Another term for a hard drive. See also Hard disk.

Interrupt An event that causes the computer to temporarily stop and perform another task.

I/O An acronym that stands for Input/Output.

Joystick A device that uses a lever to control the screen display. Often used for playing games.

Justification The placement of text or graphics between the left and right margins.

Key combinations The pressing of two keys at the same time. For example, Alt-X means to press the Alt key and hold it down, then press the X key, then release both keys at the same time.

241

Kilobyte (K) A unit of measurement that refers to 1,024 bytes.

Laptop A computer that can run off batteries and weighs less than 12 pounds. See also Luggable.

Laser printer A printer that uses light to print text and images onto paper, using the same techniques as a photocopying machine.

LCD Acronym for Liquid Crystal Display, most commonly used to describe screens that come with laptop computers.

Letter quality Refers to print quality that looks as if a typewriter printed it.

LIM Acronym for Lotus-Intel-Microsoft. Used to describe a memory specification called Expanded Memory Specification. See also EMS.

Line feed Advancing the page in a printer by one line.

Load To retrieve a file into a program such as a word processor or spreadsheet.

Local Area Network (LAN) A group of computers connected through cables, able to transfer files to other computers connected through the cables.

Luggable A term describing a computer that weighs less than 30 pounds and can be carried in one unit. See also Laptop.

Machine language A language consisting of binary data that only a computer can understand.

Macro A set of instructions that can be typed automatically by pressing a specified key combination.

Main memory Another term for random-access memory (RAM). With IBM computers, this term is used to differentiate between the first 640K in your computer (main memory), expanded memory, and extended memory.

Manual A book that contains instructions for using equipment or software. Usually loaded with typos, hard to read, and poorly organized.

Master disk The floppy disks that store programs you buy from a company.

Memory Storage inside the computer for data.

Memory-resident Term describing certain programs that copy themselves into memory and remain ready to run.

Menu A list of commands or instructions displayed on the screen. Menus are supposed to organize commands and make a program easier to use.

Menu-driven Describes a program that provides menus for choosing commands.

242

Micro Channel Architecture (MCA) IBM's proprietary design for transferring information through a computer.

Microprocessor Sometimes called the Central Processing Unit (CPU) or processor, this chip does all the calculations for the computer.

MIDI Acronym for Musical Instrument Digital Interface.

Millions of Instructions Per Second (mip) Unit of measurement to determine how fast a computer can process instructions.

Modem An acronym for MOdulator/DEModulator. A modem lets a computer send and receive data through an ordinary telephone line.

Modula-2 Programming language designed for writing complicated programs. Similar to Pascal.

Monitor A television-like display that lets the computer show information to you.

Monochrome display A monitor that can only display one color, such as green, amber, or black and white.

Motherboard The main circuit board inside the computer that every part plugs into.

Mouse A hand-held device that moves a cursor, called a mouse pointer, on the screen.

Mouse button A button on top of a mouse that performs a specific action, depending on the location of the mouse pointer on the screen.

MS-DOS The disk operating system for IBM and compatible computers.

Multitasking The ability to run more than one program simultaneously.

Multiuser The ability to let two or more people use a computer simultaneously.

Musical Instruction Digital Interface (MIDI) A standard specification for connecting sound-producing equipment, such as synthesizers, to computers.

Nanosecond A unit of measurement representing one-billionth of a second.

Network A collection of computers connected through cables. Networks are often used to share equipment, such as laser printers or hard disks.

Null modem A device that mimics a modem, used for connecting two computers together.

On-line When a printer is connected to a computer and turned on, or when a computer is connected to another computer through a modem and a telephone line.

243

On-line help Help that you can request while using a program.

Open To load a file and make it usable by a program.

Operating system A program that tells your computer how to work. Common operating systems include MS-DOS, PC DOS, and OS/2.

Page break A special code placed in a document to mark the end of a page. Used for printing word processor documents, spreadsheets, or database reports to make the printing more organized.

Pagination The numbering or ordering of pages.

Palette A selection of styles and colors available in graphics programs.

Paper size Refers to the actual size of paper. Standard sizes include letter (8 1/2 × 11 inches), legal (8 1/2 × 14 inches), European A4 (8.27 × 11.69 inches) and European B5 (6.93 × 9.84 inches).

Paper tray A device that holds paper, feeds paper into the printer, or holds paper after it emerges from the printer.

Parallel port A connector usually used to attach a printer to the computer. Often called a printer port or a parallel printer port for those who like redundancy.

Parity checking A method for detecting errors during file transmission through modems.

Partition A segment of a hard disk, usually used to divide a large hard disk into several smaller ones for faster access and organization.

Pascal A programming language designed for teaching programming. Named after the French philosopher, Blaise Pascal.

Path The route that the computer travels from the root directory to any subdirectories. The path also refers to the subdirectories that MS-DOS examines when you type a command.

Peripheral A device attached to the computer, such as a modem, disk drive, mouse, or printer.

Personal Information Manager (PIM) A category of software that organizes information you would normally write in a calendar, schedule organizer, or notebook.

Phosphor burn-in What occurs when the same image is left on the screen for extended periods of time, burning itself in so the image can be seen even when the monitor is turned off.

Pin feed A way of pushing or pulling paper through a printer by sprockets.

Pixel A dot of light that appears on the computer screen. A collection of pixels forms characters and images on the screen.

244

Platen A round rubber roller in a printer that holds paper in place.

Plotter A type of printer designed for printing color charts and graphs. A plotter uses a robotic arm for drawing an image.

Pointer An arrow-shaped icon controlled by a mouse. Used to select items on the screen such as menu commands or text.

Power supply A device that provides power to electronic equipment such as your computer. Power supplies are rated by wattage; the higher the wattage, the stronger the power supply.

Print buffer or spooler RAM memory set aside for temporarily storing data. Storing data in a print buffer lets the RAM send the data directly to the printer, freeing the computer to do something else.

Printer A device that prints data from the computer to paper.

Print head The part of the printer that strikes a ribbon against the paper.

Printout A paper copy of data printed by a printer. Also called hard copy.

Print quality The sharpness of print that a printer can produce. Print quality ranges from draft, near-letter quality (NLQ), letter quality, near-typeset quality, and typeset quality modes.

Program A series of instructions that tells the computer what to do. Typical programs are word processors, spreadsheets, databases, and games.

Programming language A set of rules for writing instructions for the computer. Popular programming languages include BASIC, C, Pascal, Modula-2, and Ada.

Prompt A symbol that the computer displays on the screen when it needs input from the keyboard.

Proportional spacing Printing or displaying characters so the left and right margins align to an arbitrary setting. Books and magazines print examples of proportional spacing with left and right margins artificially enforced to enhance the appearance of the text.

Public domain Material that is not copyrighted, and thus available for public use, free of charge.

Pull-down menu A menu display that appears at the top of the screen, organizing specific program commands into categories. Choosing a specific category displays a menu of actual program commands to select.

Pull tractor feed A device in printers that pulls paper through using sprockets and special computer paper with holes on both sides.

Push tractor feed A device in printers that pushes paper through using sprockets and special computer paper with holes on both sides.

Queue A list of messages or files waiting to reach a particular destination, such as a printer or another computer.

245

Qwerty keyboard The standard typewriter keyboard layout. The name is derived from the first six letters on the top alphabetic row of a typewriter.

Radio button A round button that appears in a dialog box, offering a choice. Only one radio button can be selected within a group of radio buttons.

RAM cache Memory set aside for temporarily holding data stored on a disk. By letting the computer access data direct from its memory (the RAM cache) instead of the disk, a RAM cache can make a computer run faster.

RAM disk Memory set aside to act like a floppy disk where you can store files. RAM disks are used to make programs run faster, like RAM caches, but a RAM disk generally uses more RAM.

Random access memory (RAM) What your computer uses to temporarily store data and programs. RAM is measured in kilobytes and megabytes. Generally the more RAM a computer has, the more capable it is.

Record Used by databases to denote a unit of information, such as someone's name, address, and phone number.

Record-locking The ability to prevent two or more people from modifying a single database record. Used with Local Area Networks (LANs).

Relational database A database program that can retrieve and manipulate data stored in two or more files. Common relational databases include dBASE III Plus, Oracle, and Paradox.

Resolution The sharpness of an image in print or on the screen. Resolution is usually measured in dots per inch (dpi) for printers and pixels for screens. The higher the resolution, the sharper the image.

RGB Acronym for Red-Green-Blue, refers to a type of color monitor.

Ribbon cable A flat cable that consists of parallel strips of wires.

ROM BIOS Acronym for Read-Only Memory, Basic Input/Output System. A special chip used to provide instructions to the computer when you turn the computer on.

RS-232 Another term for a serial port, a common standard for serial data communication between pieces of computer equipment. See also Serial port.

Scan To digitize an image or text from paper to a computer.

246

Scanner A device that converts images, such as photographs or printed text, into a format that a computer can use.

Screen The glass part of a computer monitor that displays information to the user.

Screen saver A special program that automatically blanks out your screen after a specified period of time when you do not touch the keyboard. See also Phosphor burn-in.

Scroll To move text up/down or right/left on a computer screen.

Scroll arrow An arrow displayed at the ends of each scroll bar. Clicking or holding the mouse pointer on the scroll arrow causes the document in the window to move.

Scroll bar Rectangular bars that appear on the right and bottom of a window. Clicking in the scroll bar moves the document displayed in the window.

Scroll box A box that slides in a scroll bar to indicate the relative position of a displayed document.

SCSI (Small Computer System Interface) A connector that permits communication between computers and computer peripherals such as a hard disk. SCSI devices tend to work faster than ordinary devices connected to serial or parallel ports.

Selection box A box drawn by dragging the pointer to enclose one or more graphic icons on the screen.

Serial port An interface designed to connect a computer to items like a modem, mouse, or printer. Also called an RS-232 port.

Server The main computer that controls a Local Area Network (LAN).

Shareware Programs you can legally copy and give away. If you like the program and use it, you are legally bound to send in a registration fee. In return for this fee you get a printed manual, the latest version of the program, and telephone support.

Sheet-feeder A tray that holds individual sheets of paper and slides each page into a printer one at a time.

Shell A program that lets you choose operating system commands by choosing from a menu. Shell programs try to make the computer easier to use.

Shift-click Holding down the shift key while clicking the mouse button.

SIMM (Single In-line Memory Module) A special type of RAM chip that plugs into a socket on the computer's motherboard.

Software A computer program stored on a floppy or hard disk that makes your computer do something useful, such as word processing or playing chess.

247

Source code The actual instructions of a program, written in a computer language such as BASIC, C, or Pascal.

Spike A sudden, high-intensity burst of electrical power that can damage electronic equipment including computers, stereos, and televisions. Also called power spikes or power surges.

Spreadsheet A program used for calculating numeric results. Common spreadsheets include Lotus 1-2-3, Microsoft Excel, and Quattro Pro.

Style sheet A collection of specifications for formatting text. Stylesheets may include information for font, size, style, margins, and spacing. Applying a stylesheet to text automatically formats the text according to the stylesheet's specifications.

Terminate-and-stay resident (TSR) Describes a program that resides in memory and can be used while running another program.

Trackball A device that works like an upside-down mouse. Instead of moving the mouse to move the cursor on the screen, a trackball lets you roll a ball around to move the cursor.

Tractor A belt with pins that push or pull computer paper through a printer.

Triple-click To press and release the mouse button three times rapidly in quick succession.

Trojan horse A program designed to attract your attention on the screen by displaying graphics or a fake program such as a word processor. While you watch the screen, the Trojan horse secretly erases or damages your hard disk files. See also Virus.

Undo A command that lets you take back the previous command. Some programs provide multiple undo levels, letting you take back commands you gave in the past.

Uninterruptible power supply (UPS) A battery-powered device that protects against power spikes and power outages. If the power goes out, the UPS continues supplying power to the computer so you can continue working or safely turn off your computer without losing any files.

UNIX A popular, multiuser operating system. IBM computers can use a special version called Xenix and Macintosh computers can use their own version called A/UX.

Upload To send data to another computer through a modem and a telephone line.

User-friendly Term that means that a computer or program is easy to use. Rarely used correctly.

248

Vaporware A program promised by a publisher but never released.

Virtual Graphics Array (VGA) Graphics standard for the IBM that can display 16 colors at 640 × 480 pixel resolution.

Virus A program that attaches itself to other files on a floppy or hard disk and duplicates itself without the user's knowledge. After a condition is met—the hard disk is 70% full or the date is April 1—the virus attacks the computer by erasing the hard disk. See also Trojan horse.

Wait states A condition that occurs when a processor runs faster than its memory chips can retrieve data, thereby forcing the processor to wait periodically. Fast computers have no wait states, slower computers have one or two wait states.

Word processor A program designed for turning your computer into an electronic typewriter.

Word wrap A feature that automatically moves a word to the next line if the word exceeds a predefined right margin.

Write-protect To prevent a computer from adding or modifying data stored on a disk.

Write-protect tab A small plastic tab that slides over a hole in 3 1/2-inch floppy disks, or a sticker that covers a notch cut in the side of 5 1/4-inch floppy disks.

Xmodem A method of transmitting data to another computer through modems. Transfers data in packages of 128K.

Ymodem A method of transmitting data to another computer through modems. Transfers data in packages of 1,024K, which makes it faster than the Xmodem transmission protocol.

Zoom box A box symbol that appears in the right corner of some program windows. Clicking in the zoom box causes the window to expand to fill the entire screen or to contract to a smaller size.

249

Recommended Software

With so many programs available for both IBM and Macintosh computers, finding the right program can be difficult. Every person's needs will differ, but certain programs stand out from the rest through sheer technical superiority. The program may be easy to use or offer unique features that competing programs do not include.

The following lists the names of programs that are leaders or that have earned awards for excellence. While every effort has been made to include the latest information, check software advertisements in your favorite computer magazine for the latest prices.

Relational Databases

FoxPro   *$795 (IBM)*
FoxBase+/Mac   *$395 (Macintosh)*
FoxPro and FoxBase+/Mac are completely file and command
compatible with dBASE III Plus and offer more commands and up to
fifteen times faster speed. FoxBase+/Mac lets you copy dBASE III Plus

files from an IBM to a Macintosh and use them without any modifications whatsoever.

> Fox Software
> 118 W. South Boundary
> Perrysburg, OH 43551
> (419) 874-0162

Paradox   *$795 (IBM)*

Paradox has been heralded as a powerful, easy-to-use relational database that lets beginners create complicated database programs without prior programming experience.

> Borland International
> 1700 Green Hills Road
> Scotts Valley, CA 95066-0001
> (408) 438-8400

252

4th Dimension   *$795 (Macintosh)*

4th Dimension represents one of the best relational databases available for the Macintosh. If you need to use dBASE III Plus files from an IBM, FoxBase+/Mac is a better choice.

> Acius Corporation
> 10351 Bubb Road
> Cupertino, CA 95014
> (408) 252-4444

Flat-File Databases

Q&A   *$349 (IBM)*

Q&A includes a word processor, letting you create form letters and mailing labels quickly and easily. In addition, Q&A includes a feature called the Intelligent Assistant that lets you query the database using English sentences such as, "Find me the addresses of every Smith in the state of Mississippi."

> Symantec Corporation
> 10201 Torre Avenue
> Cupertino, CA 95014
> (408) 253-9600

Reflex   *$249.95 (IBM)*

Reflex can display data in several different views that let you see relationships between data. To help you, Reflex includes graphing capabilities plus compatibility with both dBASE III Plus and Lotus 1-2-3 files.

> Borland International
> 1700 Green Hills Road
> Scotts Valley, CA 95066-0001
> (408) 438-8400

PC-File   *$129.95 (IBM)*

PC-File originally began as a shareware program but is now available commercially as well. PC-File can use data stored in dBASE III Plus files and is easier to use.

> ButtonWare
> P.O. Box 96058
> Bellevue, WA 98009
> (206) 454-0479

FileMaker Pro   *$295 (Macintosh)*

FileMaker Pro is simple for beginners to use. Currently, FileMaker Pro is the leading flat-file database for the Macintosh.

> Claris Corporation
> 440 Clyde Avenue
> Mountain View, CA 94043
> (415) 960-1500

Free-Form Databases

MemoryMate   *$69.95 (IBM)*

MemoryMate works as a memory-resident program, available to use from within any other program. It lets you store random information including letters, database records, or spreadsheets stored as text or ASCII characters.

> Broderbund Software
> 17 Paul Drive
> San Rafael, CA 94903
> (415) 492-3200

Tornado *$149.95 (IBM)*

Tornado works as a memory-resident program, available to use from within any other program. It lets you store random information including letters, database records, or spreadsheets stored as text or ASCII characters.

> MicroLogic Corporation
> P.O. Box 174
> 100 2nd Street
> Hackensack, NJ 07602
> (201) 342-6518

Desktop Publishing

PageMaker *$495 (IBM and Macintosh)*

PageMaker defined the desktop publishing field, and is widely regarded as simple for beginners to use yet powerful enough for most professionals as well. It has earned a reputation for being best for designing newsletters or flyers, but not for books or lengthy documents.

> Aldus Corporation
> 411 First Avenue S.
> Seattle, WA 98104-2871
> (206) 622-5500

Ventura Publisher *$695 (IBM and Macintosh)*

Ventura Publisher leads the desktop publishing field in the IBM market. Considered to be one of the best desktop publishing programs of all, Ventura Publisher is best for creating lengthy documents such as books or magazines, but not for creating shorter documents like brochures or flyers.

> Xerox Corporation
> 701 S. Aviation Boulevard
> El Segundo, CA 90245
> (213) 536-7000

DesignStudio *$695 (Macintosh)*
Ready,Set,Go! *$495 (Macintosh)*

DesignStudio is designed to compete as a high-end desktop publishing program for the professional. Ready,Set,Go! is designed as a powerful, but simpler program. DesignStudio's main competitor is Quark XPress. Ready,Set,Go!'s main competitor is PageMaker.

> Letraset USA
> 40 Eisenhower Drive
> Paramus, NJ 07653
> (201) 845-6100

Quark XPress   *$695 (Macintosh)*

Quark XPress is extremely popular with many Macintosh magazines such as *MacWeek*. It is considerably more powerful than PageMaker, but also more complex and expensive.

> Quark, Inc.
> 200 South Jackson
> Denver, CO 80209
> (303) 934-2211

PFS: First Publisher   *$129 (IBM)*

255

PFS: First Publisher is designed as a simple, low-end program for people who need to create simple newsletters, brochures, or flyers.

> Software Publishing Corporation
> 1901 Landings Drive
> P.O. Box 7210
> Mountain View, CA 94039-7210
> (415) 962-8910

Graphics

Harvard Presentation Graphics   *$495 (IBM)*

Harvard Presentation Graphics is the best-selling presentation graphics program for the IBM for its ease-of-use and ability to generate a wide variety of graphs.

> Software Publishing Corporation
> 1901 Landings Drive
> P.O. Box 7210
> Mountain View, CA 94039-7210
> (415) 962-8910

Freelance Plus   *$495 (IBM)*

Freelance Plus has sold on the strength of its close relationship and compatibility with the Lotus 1-2-3 spreadsheet. If you primarily use 1-2-3, then you may be more comfortable using Freelance Plus.

> Lotus Development
> 55 Cambridge Parkway
> Cambridge, MA 02142
> (617) 577-8500

Integrated Packages

Microsoft Works   *$149 (IBM)*
Microsoft Works   *$195 (Macintosh)*

Microsoft Works remains popular for its low cost, simplicity, and powerful features, including a spell checker, graphics, and communications program.

> 16011 N.E. 36th Way
> Box 97017
> Redmond, WA 98073-9717
> (206) 882-8080

PFS: First Choice   *$149 (IBM)*

PFS: First Choice remains popular for its low cost, simplicity, and powerful features, including a spell checker, graphics, and communications program.

> Software Publishing Corporation
> 1901 Landings Drive
> P.O. Box 7210
> Mountain View, CA 94039-7210
> (415) 962-8910

Framework III   *$695 (IBM)*

Framework III is an extremely powerful integrated package. The word processor portion offers many advanced features of dedicated word

processors such as WordPerfect, and the spreadsheet portion of
Framework III is as powerful as Lotus 1-2-3.

> Ashton-Tate
> 20101 Hamilton Avenue
> Torrance, CA 90502-1319
> (213) 329-8000

Language Compilers

Microsoft BASIC   *$495 (IBM)*
Microsoft C   *$495 (IBM)*
Microsoft Macro Assembler   *$149 (IBM)*
QuickBASIC   *$99 (IBM and Macintosh)*
QuickC   *$99 (IBM)*

257

Microsoft BASIC, C, and Macro Assembler have set the standard for
language compilers. For novice programmers, Microsoft offers
QuickBASIC and QuickC, which provide many features of Microsoft's
professional compilers but at a much lower cost.

> Microsoft Corporation
> 16011 N.E. 36th Way
> Box 97017
> Redmond, WA 98073-9717
> (206) 882-8080

Consulair Development System
> **68000 Assembler**   *$79.95 (Macintosh)*
> **68020/68030 Assembler**   *$130 (Macintosh)*

Consulair Development System is one of the few assemblers available
for the Macintosh. The assembler comes in two versions: one for the
older Macintosh Plus and SE computers, and a second for the newer
Macintosh II computers.

> Consulair Development
> P.O. Box 2192
> Ketchum, ID 83340
> (208) 726-5846

Think C *$249 (Macintosh)*
Think Pascal *$249 (Macintosh)*

Think C and Think Pascal are the most popular language compilers for the Macintosh. Most popular programs, including FoxBase+/Mac and PageMaker, were written using Think C or Think Pascal.

>   Symantec Corporation
>   10201 Torre Avenue
>   Cupertino, CA 95014
>   (408) 253-9600

Turbo C *$149 (IBM)*
Turbo Pascal *$149 (IBM)*
Turbo Pascal *$99 (Macintosh)*
Turbo Assembler *$149 (IBM)*

258

Turbo C, Turbo Pascal, and Turbo Assembler are direct competitors to Microsoft's language compilers. Turbo Pascal has set the standard for Pascal compilers for the IBM. Turbo C runs faster and provides more help for novice C programmers. Turbo Assembler assembles programs faster than Microsoft's Macro Assembler.

>   Borland International
>   1700 Green Hills Road
>   Scotts Valley, CA 95066-0001
>   (408) 438-8400

TopSpeed C *$199 (IBM)*
TopSpeed C++ *$199 (IBM)*
TopSpeed Modula−2 *$199 (IBM)*
TopSpeed Pascal *$199 (IBM)*

TopSpeed C, TopSpeed C++, TopSpeed Modula−2, and TopSpeed Pascal were written by former employees of Borland International who worked on the original Turbo Pascal. All the TopSpeed compilers work together so you can write programs combining C, Pascal, and Modula−2.

>   Jensen and Partners International
>   1101 San Antonio Road, Suite 301
>   Mountain View, CA 94043
>   (415) 967-3200

Spreadsheets

Lotus 1-2-3   *$595 (IBM)*

Lotus 1-2-3 version 3.0 is designed for IBM AT or compatible computers and includes the ability to create three-dimensional spreadsheets. Lotus 1-2-3 version 2.2 is designed for the older IBM PC/XT computers but cannot create three-dimensional spreadsheets.

> Lotus Development
> 55 Cambridge Parkway
> Cambridge, MA 02142
> (617) 577-8500

Microsoft Excel   *$495 (IBM and Macintosh)*

Microsoft Excel has long been considered superior to Lotus 1-2-3 for its large number of features and excellent graphing capabilities. Available for both the IBM and Macintosh, Microsoft Excel lets you share data files between two computers.

259

> Microsoft Corporation
> 16011 N.E. 36th Way
> Box 97017
> Redmond, WA 98073-9717
> (206) 882-8080

Quattro Pro   *$495 (IBM)*

Quattro Pro is a direct competitor to Lotus 1-2-3. Unlike Lotus 1-2-3, Quattro Pro can run on a standard IBM PC/XT.

> Borland International
> 1700 Green Hills Road
> Scotts Valley, CA 95066-0001
> (408) 438-8400

VP-Planner 3D   *$249 (IBM)*

VP-Planner 3D provides a five-dimensional spreadsheet with dBASE III Plus file creation and loading abilities. For extensive consolidation needs, VP-Planner 3D proves superior to most other spreadsheets on the market.

> Paperback Software
> 2830 Ninth Street
> Berkeley, CA 94710
> (415) 644-2116

WingZ   *$399 (Macintosh)*

WingZ provides its own programming language called HyperScript, enabling you to create your own custom applications. Like Quattro Pro, WingZ also offers an extensive range of capabilities, including color and three-dimensional graphics.

> Informix Software
> 4100 Bohannon Drive
> Menlo Park, CA 94025
> (415) 322-0573

Full Impact   *$295 (Macintosh)*

Full Impact offers nearly as many features as WingZ, but has not been marketed as aggressively. Full Impact provides many presentation capabilities for creating reports.

> Ashton-Tate
> 20101 Hamilton Avenue
> Torrance, CA 90502-1319
> (213) 329-8000

260

Utilities

The Norton Utilities   *$99 (IBM)*

The Norton Utilities has set the standard for utility programs. Easy to use, yet powerful for beginners and experienced computer owners, The Norton Utilities can protect your files from almost any disaster.

> Peter Norton Computing, Inc.
> 100 Wilshire Boulevard
> Suite 900
> Santa Monica, CA 90403
> (213) 826-8032

PC Tools Deluxe   *$129 (IBM)*
MacTools Deluxe   *$129 (Macintosh)*

PC Tools Deluxe offers as many features as The Norton Utilities, but with the addition of a simple word processor, database, and telecommunications program combined with easy-to-use menus.

MacTools Deluxe is the Macintosh version of PC Tools Deluxe but without the word processor, database, and telecommunications portion.

>Central Point Software
>15220 N.W. Greenbrier Parkway
>Suite 200
>Beaverton, OR 97006
>(503) 690-8090

The Mace Utilities *$129 (IBM)*

The Mace Utilities is more difficult to use than either The Norton Utilities or PC Tools Deluxe, but is unrivaled in its disk recovery abilities. You can format a disk and The Mace Utilities can still recover all your data. If you need the best in file recovery, then The Mace Utilities is the best program for the job.

>Fifth Generation Systems
>11200 Industrialplex Boulevard
>Baton Rouge, LA 70809-4112
>(504) 291-7221

261

Word Processors

WordPerfect *$495 (IBM, Macintosh, Atari ST, Amiga)*

WordPerfect has become the standard for IBM word processing. To make the program more accessible to beginners, the latest version of WordPerfect includes pull-down menus and mouse support. WordPerfect offers one of the best telephone support policies in the industry with toll-free numbers you can call for help.

>WordPerfect Corporation
>1555 N. Technology Way
>Orem, UT 84057
>(801) 225-5000

Microsoft Word   *$495 (IBM)*
Word for Windows   *$495 (IBM)*
Microsoft Word   *$395 (Macintosh)*

Microsoft Word and Word for Windows are rival programs to
WordPerfect. Microsoft Word is also available for the IBM and
Macintosh, letting you easily share data between the two computers.

Microsoft Corporation
16011 N.E. 36th Way
Box 97017
Redmond, WA 98073-9717
(206) 882-8080

WriteNow   *$195 (Macintosh)*

WriteNow is one of the least expensive Macintosh word processors, but
also one of the fastest and easiest to use. In addition, WriteNow
requires the least amount of memory of any Macintosh word processor.

T/Maker Company
1390 Villa Street
Mountain View, CA 94041
(415) 962-0195

Index

264

265

266

267

268

269

270

271

273

Reader Feedback Card

Thank you for purchasing this book from Howard W. Sams & Company's FIRST BOOK series. Our intent with this series is to bring you timely, authoritative information that you can reference quickly and easily. You can help us by taking a minute to complete and return this card. We appreciate your comments and will use the information to better serve your needs.

1. Where did you purchase this book?

☐ Chain bookstore (Walden, B. Dalton)   ☐ Direct mail
☐ Independent bookstore   ☐ Book club
☐ Computer/Software store   ☐ School bookstore
☐ Other _____

2. Why did you choose this book? (Check as many as apply.)

☐ Price   ☐ Appearance of book
☐ Author's reputation   ☐ Howard W. Sam's reputation
☐ Quick and easy treatment of subject   ☐ Only book available on subject

3. How do you use this book? (Check as many as apply.)

☐ As a supplement to the product manual   ☐ As a reference
☐ In place of the product manual   ☐ At home
☐ For self-instruction   ☐ At work

4. Please rate this book in the categories below. G = Good; N = Needs improvement; U = Category is unimportant.

☐ Price   ☐ Appearance
☐ Amount of information   ☐ Accuracy
☐ Examples   ☐ Quick Steps
☐ Inside cover reference   ☐ Second color
☐ Table of contents   ☐ Index
☐ Tips and cautions   ☐ Illustrations
☐ Length of book
☐ How can we improve this book? _____

5. How many computer books do you normally buy in a year?

☐ 1—5   ☐ 5—10   ☐ More than 10
☐ I rarely purchase more than one book on a subject.
☐ I may purchase a beginning and an advanced book on the same subject.
☐ I may purchase several books on particular subjects.
(such as _____)

6. Have you purchased other Howard W. Sams or Hayden books in the past year? ___
If yes, how many? _____

7. Would you purchase another book in the FIRST BOOK series? _____

8. What are your primary areas of interest in business software?
   - ☐ Word processing (particularly _____)
   - ☐ Spreadsheet (particularly _____)
   - ☐ Database (particularly _____)
   - ☐ Graphics (particularly _____)
   - ☐ Personal finance/accounting (particularly _____)
   - ☐ Other (please specify _____)

Other comments on this book or the Howard W. Sams book line: _____
_____

Name _____
Company _____
Address _____
City _____ State _____ Zip _____
Daytime telephone number _____
Title of this book _____

Fold here

‖‖‖‖

BUSINESS REPLY MAIL
FIRST CLASS   PERMIT NO. 336   CARMEL, IN

POSTAGE WILL BE PAID BY ADDRESSEE

Sams

11711 N. College Ave.
Suite 140
Carmel, IN 46032–9839

ՍՍՍՍՍՍՍՍՍՍՍՍՍՍՍՍՍՍՍՍՍ